A Cowboy's Family and Friends

Memories of a Cowboy Poet

Second Edition

Poems by
Leroy L. Davis
and Friends

Illustrations by
Kimberly O'Neall Williams

Published by
Becky Davis Smith

Published as a labor of love by
Becky Davis Smith.

Sales inquiries should be directed to
Becky Davis Smith
becky@nobsranch.com.

Library of Congress Control Number: 2009909079

International Standard Book Number (ISBN): 978-0-615-33105-8

Printed in the United States of America

Dedicated to the last of the real cowboys and to my father, whose experiences and talent gave rise to this book. I must say that I have learned more about my father after reading his poems than I had ever previously known.

This second edition contains all of the poems from the first edition along with more poems written by my father and others that Dad wanted to include.

Thank you, Dad, for sharing your memories with us.

Becky Davis Smith

Acknowledgements

This collection of my father's poems came into my possession a few years ago. I had intended at that time to publish them for my father, but soon learned that self-publishing was a costly exercise.

Today, new options are available for aspiring poets and authors at an affordable price. When I discovered Lulu.com, I knew that the time had finally come to realize the dream of publishing this book for my father.

Special thanks to Norman Kolpas of Kolpas Media for taking time from an already busy schedule to proofread and format these pages.

Another thank-you to KingRidge, LLC. (_www.KingRidge.org_) for the cover design.

Haven't Sold Your Saddle by Waddie Mitchell is used by permission, Waddie's Word Publishing.

If This Old Tack Could Talk by Brad Hall is reprinted from The Fence Post.

Unless otherwise noted on individual poems, all of these are original works by my father, Leroy Davis. This book is for you, Dad.

Contents

Leroy

Here's a little story
About a man named Leroy.
A "Cuttin' horse man,"
Just the best in the land
Is "Ole Leroy"!
All loaded with spurs, saddles, and horse,
He's gone again to take a first.

After the chores, and kissin' "Sis" goodnight,
He'll take to the barn.
He's got something to write.
Might stay till early light,
Could be longer if it don't sound just right.

His stories are short, and they rhyme, you see.
He has a talent you wouldn't believe.
Writes of his folks and family,
The "Good Lord above,"
Maybe you or me.

We won't know for sure
Till it's all complete,
Cause he'll keep it a secret.
Won't give us a peek.

Then he'll call us all in,
With a silly little grin,
He'll hand us a beer,
We'll all settle in.

Cause we all know
Before Leroy reads us the end,
We'll have tears in our eyes
Or a "silly little grin."

Written by Sherrie Ann Glenn

Horseshoeing Deception

I've got this gentle halter horse I want you to shoe.
They tell me you are the best so it has got to be you.
With all these compliments and praise coming down,
I tell him I will, first time I get around.

The next morning, at just the break of dawn,
I drive to his place, and should not be long.
Looking through the fence, he is kinda a sorry cuss,
But I'll treat him with kindness, so there will
    be no fuss.

With my tools all out, and my shoeing apron on,
I go to catch that dishwater roan.
He came to me, just pretty as you please,
I lead him out thinking, This will be a breeze.

Forty-five minutes, if I stop for a smoke,
And less time than that, if he is really broke.
I rub his neck and say, "What a pretty man."
I guess he knew I was lying, 'cause he sure got mad.

I reached to pick up a dirty front foot,
And his ears went back, as he reached for my butt.
I knew right then, I hadn't been told everything.
The way they lie about their horses, sure
    seems strange.

But I know a trick or two. For this old horse
I'll put a twitch on his lip, to get him on course.
I get it on all right, as he stood real still,
But when I reached for his foot, he tried to kill.

He set back so hard, I thought my halter would break.
Right then I knew, this horse was kinda rank.
He reared and went just as high as he could go,
Then pawed at the air, every way but slow.

I reached real quick and grabbed for the twitch,
He came so close to my head, it began to itch.
I walked to my pickup, to have a smoke,
And when I finished, I reached for my rope.

What he really needed, was laying down,
As I reached for a back foot, he came unwound.
But after a lot of cussin', sweat, and dust,
I laid him down so hard, I thought he would bust.

Now shoeing's not easy, when they are upside down,
But there ain't no dang horse, gonna make me
   a clown.
This job started at dawn, and it is way past noon,
I'm thinking about getting paid, and real dang soon.

I go back to this man, that gave me the praise,
And try to hide my eyes, so he won't see the craze.
"How did ole Honey Boy do?" he asked with
   a smile.
"He is just the kind I like," I lied for a while.

"He was nice, sweet, and gentle, as you please,
And really likes it when you play with his knees.
If you need him shod again, just give me a ring.
And if I'm not too busy, I'll shoe that pretty thing."

Right then and there I knew, in the back of my mind,
I would never be hungry enough, to shoe that kind.
I felt I had gotten even, with my little white lie,
But the next guy to shoe ole Honey will be in a bind.

The Cowboy

My Uncle Francis

He made his living with a horse, a rope, and a saddle.
There never was a horse Ole Frank couldn't straddle.
    He could use a rope like an extension of this arm,
Whether doctoring worms or branding hot iron.

When working a pasture, he knew every angle.
He earned his beans many years for the
  old "Triangle. "
Wagon time and branding time was what he
  liked best.
A cowboy's cowboy, a little better than the rest.

When the gather was made, if they were big
  and rank,
Catch that good horse, and give the rope to old Frank.
In the branding pen, whether they was big or small,
Using a little bell loop, you could hear it squall.

He could drag 'em all day, without ever a miss,
You could see it on his face, the heavenly bliss.
This was the life he loved; he would trade with
  no one.
Being a cowboy to him was just having fun.

He worked for the matador, "Turtle Hole" was
  the place,
Just a little line camp where you set your own pace.
A wood cook stove, and coal oil for light,
They had no television to mess up their night.

To bed by sundown, and up before dawn,
Check that remuda and cut out the roan.
There were miles to ride and cattle to see,
Check all the waters and see how they be.

Friends call him "Puss, " but that was all in fun,
When it came to hurrahing, he could make 'em
all run.
Way back in the thirties, when times were real hard,
Francis broke wild mustangs for old Puttard Boyd.

The pay wasn't real great, just five dollars a head,
But he had to do it to keep his family fed.
He could ride a bronc like few men I've known,
Sunfishing, high diving, and bad to the bone.

Ole Frank could fan 'em and laugh every jump,
He could spur 'em in the shoulder and kick 'em
in the rump.
Born in a covered wagon back in 1903,
He would spend his life horseback, a cowboy
he would be.

The Sixes, Pitchforks, Triangles, and ole Matador,
He worked for them all, not far from Seymour.
With a burden to bear for half of his life,
The one he loved most was his invalid wife.

He cared for her and loved her as long as she lived,
Hope had faded long ago that she could ever be well.
Just this August, and the year is '89,
"Ole Frank" went to meet her, so I know
they are fine.

Together forever, they are handsome and young,
Laughing and talking and singing,
the old songs they had sung.
He's still a cowboy though, but don't get it wrong,
Ole Frank's not like the ones you hear in a song.

He was the real thing, and if you missed him
that's sad.
I know he was the best uncle, a nephew ever had.

Lonely Cowboy

The north wind blows,
Tumbleweeds are prowling.
In the dark of the night,
A hungry coyote is howling.

A whippoorwill calls,
Searching for its mate.
Hoping to find her
Before it's too late.

The moon up there
Is shining down on me,
Telling me of someone
I would sure like to see.

You notice these things,
When you are all alone.
Wondering about your
   loved one,
Wishing she could come home.

Is she safe and warm
Wherever she is at?
Does she ever think of me
In this old brown hat?

Have the miles made
   a difference
In the way she feels?
Would she like to be here?
Is her love for me real?

Has this cowboy become,
Just an old dull thing?
If she had a chance,
Would she still take my name?

This cowboy's life,
Can sure be lonely.
When you are home alone,
Without your one and only.

November 22, 1989

The Jim Reno Trophy

The first of its kind to come along,
The perfect picture: of a cowboy, on his throne.
Everyone wants one, but they are not for sale.
You have to win it, and that's a long trail.

I will describe it for you; it's a sight to see,
A cow trying to get by a horse, but he won't let her flee.
A long yearling heifer, as her horns will show,
The cutting horse has got her; by him she won't blow.

Down low in front, he is working eye to eye.
She will not run by him, no matter what the try.
The cowboy pilot sure looks like a hand to me,
Sittin' straight, legs down, with a little bend at the knee.

The mane is flying and the tail all a' swirl,
Little ears are forward and body a' curl.
Front feet all forward, and back ones also,
It's the perfect cuttin' horse trophy, designed by Jim Reno.

First Time Bronc Rider

I just left the farm, but none of it shows,
Cause I'm all dressed up in these new Western clothes.
I'm wearing my best, and in case you can't tell,
When I get through with this rodeo, I'll have money to sell.

I plan to start small, till I get real good,
So I figure the place to start would be ole Clarkwood.
I hit town about noon and it's plain to see
This town is wide open, just waiting for me.

I park my old flivver, and find me a room
To lie down and rest, cause rodeo time is soon.
Now the waiting time is over and I'm ready to go
Down to fair park and the big rodeo.

They're all gathered 'round the chutes, waitin' for the draw.
They pull out my number, and he's a real outlaw.
The Grand Entry is over, and they carry the colors.
My riggin's cinched up, and I'm ready for this old scutter.

They started with chute number one, but mine is number nine.
I'll handle this old nag just like he was mine.
They move right along, and it's plain to see
The next cowboy out is bound to be me.

I get down on him, just like an old pro.
You better believe me, I'm aiming to show.
I nod my head once, and the gate swings wide.
Get out of the way boys and I'll show you a ride.

The going is sure rough, but I'm still astraddle.
I believe I have a chance at that pretty trophy saddle.
A bucking and bawling, and dust everywhere.
I could ride this old outlaw in Paw's underwear.

I decide if I win it, I'll have to get wild,
So start to spur hard, and he really gets riled.
Six seconds have passed, and it seems like a week,
My insides are churning right down to my feet.

16

This ole hoss can sure pitch, and that ain't no lie.
If I come loose now, I'll be flying through the sky.
I have lost one stirrup, and my timing is all gone,
My head is a'spinnin, and I let out a groan.

The ground comes up to meet me, right in the face,
And I lay here and wonder, "Where is this place?"
The lights are so bright, and the voices are so loud,
Everything is blurred, like seeing through a cloud.

I shake my head hard, and shake off the dirt,
Then stand up slow to see if I'm hurt.
There's no broken bones, as far as I can tell,
So throw back my head and let out a yell.

I've lost this contest, but it's plain to see,
A real rodeo champion I aim to be.

My Cuttin' Hoss

He's a sight to see and a joy to own.
Riding this good one is like sittin' on a throne.
Whether it's Poco, Doc, Little Oakie, or Cutter,
In front of a cow he's going to flutter.

So smart and wise and eager to please,
If a cow really tries him, he'll get on his knees.
Calm on the outside, you can feel his heart pound.
When a cow gets tough, he'll tear up the ground.

This way and that way, without even a cue,
Bring her on boys; he knows what to do.
He explodes one way, and back to the other.
Let's finish this cow and get us another.

This run's been a good one; don't mess up now.
Let's ease back in the herd for one last cow.
I'll pick you a good one, that black baldy will do.
When she's clear of the herd, it's all up to you.

We're marking in the seventies with time left to spare,
Just work this last one right down to the hair.
I hear the whistle blow, so it's all over now.
Probably all that judge will be able to say is, "Wow!"

They call out the score and to my surprise,
It's a sixty some odd, with no compromise.
That judge has got to be blind, is all I can say,
He has gone and ruined my very best day.

I'll take this ole hoss home and teach him some more,
Bring him back a little later and make a seventy-four.

Gay Doc's Spot

We call him Gay Doc, but now don't you laugh.
You put him on a cow, and just watch his gas.
He's just real quick, but little in stature,
The way he can move could sure cause a fracture.

He was bred just right, by the great "Gay Bar King, "
With all kinds of good horses in between.
His mother was so noble, with the Doc Bar blood,
You wouldn't change her pedigree, even if you could.

He is roan in color, with a lot of white hair,
With four high white stockings, sure gives him a flair.
A big star and stripe in the center of his face,
And little pin ears in just the right place.

He is quite a stud also, as his babies will show.
Just like their daddy, we got two in a row.
Little fox ears and big protruding, pretty eyes,
They are both just dandy, a gal and a guy.

We showed him this year, and to no one's surprise,
He is a fighter and a winner, with no compromise.
Just put him in a class and if there's any doubt,
You can ask him to get tough; he knows what it's about.

Doc can work a cow, with no more than a halter,
Just cut the herd clean and he'll never falter.
He will explode to the left, and then back to the right.
Sit there and ride him, but hold on tight.

He is taking you for a ride, as everyone can see.
Just sit there and ride him, but let him be.
He knows what he is doing and needs little help from you,
Don't get in his way or give him the wrong cue.

He can do it on instinct, cause he's got the blood,
And he knows more about a cow than man ever could.
I really like this little horse and the way he can move,
Head down, with feet pawing, to stay in the groove.

He will never cold trail, and then run right past her,
If they want to get fast, he can sure get faster.
They don't have a chance, with his big eyes a'buggin,
Such an easy mover, never heavy and a'luggin.

I sound like a grandpa, all swaggering and bragging,
But I just love ole Gay Doc when his bottom's a dragging.
I've had a lot of good horses between these two knees,
But none quite like this little stud, so eager to please.

Just lucky to own him, cause he makes my day,
There will never be another one quite like little Gay.

Old Brown Hat

This old hat of mine
Has sure seen a lot.
It's been tramped
  on the floor
And folded in the cot.

Stepped on in the bronc pen,
And soaked in the rain.
Run over by a lot of cattle,
And tipped to a lot of Janes.

I bought it twelve years ago
For fifty nine or eight,
The saleswoman said it was
  a good one,
And on me, it sure
  looked great.

A brown hat's my color,
So that's what I got.
But after a few mishaps,
This hat's took the rot.

I used to brush it off,
With just a swish of
  the broom,
Here lately it seems
This hat's lost its bloom.

I wear it every day
Cause it feels just fine.
It's not very pretty anymore,
    It's started to recline.

Maybe I could re-do it
With some soap and water.
Maybe use this wire brush
To knock off the fodder.

Whatever it takes
To put it back in style,
I sure aim to do it.
I want to keep it awhile.

It's broke in just right,
And sure fits my head.
Ridin' these cutting horses,
It sticks just like lead.

They don't make
  them anymore,
Quite like they used to.
I've heard it said many times,
Your hat looks just like you.

November 25, 1989

A Cowboy

You can distinguish a cowboy by his walk and his talk.
Maybe it's his jeans, or is it his cowboy stalk?
Don't ask me how, but there's one thing for sure,
You don't make a cowboy from a five-and-dime store.

Maybe it's seasoning in the great open space,
From living the good life, that shows on his face.
The outside of a horse is good for the inside of a man.
May they always be with us to look after this land.

The cowboys have got it; you can see it in their eye.
Just like a great horse, they have plenty to try.
They have pride in their veins like a great thoroughbred.
Under that big hat, common sense in their head.

A cowboy will shake your hand, but it's not just a token.
If he gives you his word, it will never be broken.
The legend has been here all these many years,
And told so many times through heartache and tears.

"Little Joe, The Wrangler, " killed in that awful stampede,
The Pony Express rider, who was barely fifteen.
He is not just a rodeo rider, though some are the best.
You might see a cowboy anywhere; they are not all out West.

November 15, 1989

Retired Cowboy

Always a cowboy, so that's all he knew,
Jobs open to him now are seldom and few.
A rough string rider, when young and strong,
Thinking about it now doesn't seem that long.

Years pass fast when you are young and free,
With a good horse to ride and cattle to see.
He never owned a cow, but that bothered him none.
Working the boss's cows to him was just fun.

There were always young horses to ride.
The best hand around, he could teach 'em to slide.
Rough hands like velvet, he never hurt a mouth,
When it came to making a cow horse, there was no drought.

Just sitting there thinking, about the roan or the gray,
About the good feeling of a high stepping bay.
Reliving the past now is about all he has,
Without the good memories life would be sad.

An old bunkhouse had always been home.
He remembered them all as he let his thoughts roam.
Never a large wardrobe to keep in style,
A clean shirt and blue jeans could make him smile.

Long retired now and living in town,
Staying at the biggest bunkhouse to be found.
Don't tell it like it is, cause this is his throne,
His pride would never let him stay in an old folk's home.

June 7, 1991

Old Zack

Larry had him first, just a bundle of fun,
Playing in the floor or the yard, always at a run.
Zack just a pup, all fluffy and clean,
You could never imagine old Zack could be mean.

He grew up knowing the people he would love,
For those loved ones he had the heart of a dove.
Mostly German Shepard, with the mind of a saint,
When you hear him at night, you better stop and think.

What did I do wrong this time? Didn't I close that gate?
It's the middle of the night, and Zack says it can't wait.
Such a dear friend, so loyal and true,
We love you Zack. When you're gone, what will we do?

He is old now, can't hear or hardly see,
But don't tell him that, cause he still runs this place, the DND.
When anything happens that's just not right,
Old Zack will tell you, be it day or night.

We run a horse operation here on this dusty five,
And Zack won't put up with no funny stuff or jive.
It's all business with him, when feeding time comes,
You better not be late either, putting feed in those drums.

The cats like to fight, oh how the fur can fly.
But old Zack won't let this happen around him, they get shy.
There's just one man old Zack doesn't trust,
That UPS man and his little green bus.

Now he'll bring our packages, but he won't get out.
Old Zack sees to that, he acts like a scout.
He'll chase that truck till it's clean out of sight,
Running and barking with all of his might.

When a young dog, and in his prime,
He proved to his mistress he was worth her time.
She was moving from Colorado to eastern New Mexico
When her pick-up stopped, it just wouldn't go.

She sat there and waited for help to arrive,
When this load of rednecks pulled up, to her surprise.
They was up to no good, it was plain to see,
Old Zack sensed it too as he lay on her knee.

Up like a shot with his hair all a'bristle,
Those local yokels loaded and left like a whistle.
Zack, you've got a home here for a long time we hope,
We'll love you and keep you forever, no joke.

You can be the boss, and keep us in line,
Because, should you leave, we'd be in a bind.
Who would watch this place at night while we sleep?
Or boss in the morning, when we're late to feed?

Though you are half blind and can hardly see,
You can do it on instinct, and that's good enough for me.
When you are gone and no longer around,
You will still be at home, on DND ground.

Dolores and Me

We got this place started in the fall of eighty-five,
A cutting, halter horse operation, just trying to survive.
We started real small, with a "let's wait and see...."
The only two good cowboys around was Dolores and me.

This job's seven days a week, cause horses have to eat,
And if you ride 'em and slide 'em, you take care
    of their feet.
Up early every morning and clean all those stalls,
Clean that wash rack, rake everywhere, and
    wet down those halls.

With the chores all done, it's now time to ride.
Dolores starts her halter babies; we work side by side.
There's shows coming up and we'd like to do good.
I had better work ole "Magic," so I cinch on my wood.

I put him on the walker, to take off the top,
Then saddle ole "Poco," I need to help with his stop.
Each one is different and no two trains alike.
These are thinking horses and you don't ride them
    like a bike.

Repetition is the answer, be kind, gentle, but stern.
Get in his mind, think like he thinks, and help him to learn.
He is the pride of the West and the talk of the town,
No other animal can match him, there's just none around.

No cow can out-think him or stay with his pace.
She tries to out run him and she just lost that race.
He works on his own, with little help from you.
Get a cow in front of him and he knows what to do.

I've worked six today but it's not over yet.
There's still chores to do and wash off that sweat.
Plait up those tails, so they will be long for the shows.
When we get them to town, we want them to glow.

"Winning is not everything," is what I've often heard
    and said.
But everything is winning, or soon you'll be dead.

That halter horse is a good one, but it's who leads him
    that counts.
You stand him up perfect, or the judge turns you out.

Now my partner does this better than anyone I know.
When she gets one ready, he'll be ready to show.
There's no detail too small and no job that's too hard.
You can tell it in the show ring as she gets her reward.

We have had a few heartaches, but we've moved right along.
Life has its ups and downs, everything's not a song.
Ole Lady lost her baby and Tracey did the same.
Satin Secrets died of colic, and Oakie came up lame.

Priss was supposed to have a baby, but none could be found.
We watched and waited for Barbee, but she made us
    a clown.
What waits for us in the future, we'll have to wait and see.
Whatever comes our way, we sure can handle it,
    Dolores and me.

We have had our fusses, more than one or two,
But she is still my partner, and we will see it through.
I like it fine the way it is, just Dolores and me.
We have turned this place into something, it's "The DND."

A Sinner's Prayer

This life is half over,
It has been one big sin.
Should the Master call me
Like this, I could never win.

It wasn't always like this,
I want you to know.
My life was good and clean,
And the bad didn't show.

How and why did it
    all happen?
I hear myself say.
I guess I will ask myself that
Until my dying day.

When I was younger
    and eager,
And so full of fun,
Lord I never forgot
That you were the one.

You were my guiding light,
And so bright did you shine.
If only I had followed
    that light,
I would have never been
    so blind.

The pitfalls of life,
Are so dark, and so deep,
The mountains to
    everlasting life,
Seem so long and so steep.

My Mother and Daddy
    have gone
To be with you now.
Lord, I ask you on my knees,
Please, let me be with them
    someday, somehow.

I loved them so much,
But that was no sin.
When you called them
    that day,
I gave up my dearest kin.

They are walking up
    there slowly,
Just waiting for me.
I pray I can catch them,
Lord, I ask you on my knee.

This life you gave me
Through them, I have wasted.
It is half gone,
But more than half wasted.

March 15, 1979

30

The Wedding

About this time of year, not too long ago,
I met this angel, and I knew I could love her so.
Everything happened pretty fast, and wouldn't you know?
About three months later, we had the big show.

A horseback wedding was what we would have,
With friends and relatives from everywhere,
   enough to fill a town.
They came from far and near that day, just to see us
Stand in front of that preacher and say, "We Trust."

A more beautiful bride you will never see,
Riding a white Paint mare, so pretty and clean.
With roses on her breast collar, placed just right,
Her brown eyes were smiling and her hair so light.

All the people were watching her, such a beautiful sight.
Twelve people were horseback, all dressed in their best.
Let's have a horseback wedding was her request.
With catering service, a band, two kegs of beer, and
   all the rest.

We did have a wedding that day, not too long ago.
It was for real, though, and not just for show.
When she looked at me and said, "Till death do us part,"
I repeated after that preacher with all of my heart.

With the wedding all over and just living to do,
Life looked real good, the skies were so blue.
A honeymoon was in order, so where should we go?
Nashville, we decided, for the Grand Old Opry show.

What a place it was, with all of its stars,
Roy Acuff, George Jones, and a hundred guitars.
We saw it all, I guess, on that honeymoon trip,
But the nights were the best, when we were lip to lip.

Thrilled by your love, to think you chose me
To share your life, and your partner to be.
I may come up short sometimes, I suppose,
But to you my heart's door will never close.

For some things I have said, apologies have waited too long,
Just like a kiss, once you give it, it's gone.
You are my strength, the light of my life,
A joy to my heart and soul, my darling wife.

I will keep you in sickness, in health or in pain,
Being with you and near you will never be in vain.
I guess being your hero is what I want to be,
A great warrior, or maybe Romeo, on one knee.

Standing real tall and brave and clean,
Or maybe a macho man, like Rambo, and mean.
Whatever you like, fat, skinny, or lean,
Just let me be the one you love, and cling.

I can't be like the others, who have loved you and lost,
But I will try to please you, no matter the cost.
Two people together, trying to be one,
Laughing, loving, and caring, that's the fun.

It's not near over yet, and I'm still hanging tight.
As long as we have love, we will be all right.

Annie Velma Glenn

Andrew had this homestead that he wanted to prove,
So he asked Velma to marry him, and she made the move.
They were just a young ranch couple starting out
   on their own.
All they wanted was a family, and to own their own home.

This first house he had for her was just a one-room shack,
But she fixed it up real pretty from front to back.
Bedroom, dining room, kitchen, and parlor, all in one,
But when you are young and in love, a one-room house
   can be fun

They lived there a few years, but needed more room
To start and raise their family, and watch them bloom.
They bought the Crosby house, not far from the first site.
Their life was so good, and the future looked so bright.

Through good and bad years, they managed to survive.
The happiest time for Velma was when a new baby arrived.
She got just what she wanted, and the number was nine.
This would keep her busy for many years, and take
   all her time.

I have talked to her many times about life and how it was,
And those stories she has told me, I treasure every one.
The one I like best, and I will tell it to you,
About how she felt about Heaven, and it's all true.

"I wouldn't mind Heaven, and I know it wouldn't be bad,
But if I could just know it would be as good as I've had."
She told me this, not too long ago,
As we talked about Heaven, and the great afterglow.

About the life she lived just for her husband and her kids,
And about the life "UP THERE," where it really
   begins again.
Andrew went on before her, just to fix up that place,
And he is watching and waiting, at a real slow pace.

They were always ranchers, and cattle they raised,
Getting by and raising their family with very little praise.
Andrew the cowman, and Velma the homemaker,
She was the cook, dishwasher, bookkeeper, seamstress,
    and baker.

She didn't mind the chores, though a thousand and one.
When you love your family, you stay on the run.
She would help Andrew when needed, like pull a cow
    from the bog,
Or go with him to the pasture if it was misty or fog.

They worked as a team, but the cow work was his.
She kept the house, and cooked, for nine hungry kids.
Up before daylight, to get them off to school,
There was no time to be a busybody or lay around a pool.

She had a family to raise, and this she did well.
Never a large bank account, to sit and watch swell.
It took all they had just to kinda get by.
There was always clothes to buy and food to supply.

She took pride in her kids and all they could do
Just happy being family, her skies always seemed blue.
Then tragedy struck one day and her son Kenny was taken,
The strong one she was, though her heart was breaking.

This grieved her so much, but she still had eight.
Life had taught her patience, so she would have to wait
To see him again on that other shore,
When they would be together again, just like before.

A few years later, tragedy was to strike again.
Another son was lost in an accident, not far from Belen.
After this she knew it would never be like before,
Until they all got together again on that other shore.

Her life had been so good, and she never did wrong.
She just kept the faith and moved right along,
Always accepting her life as being God's will,
And the way she could accept things is quite a thrill.

With her family raised and all of them gone,
She was now the rancher, she had turned every stone.
Always the homemaker, until her family was raised,
And now the cow woman with cattle to graze.

Just a real rare woman to do all of these things,
Taking care of her family, then working the range.
Put out those protein blocks, and see about the salt.
Her truck stalls on the backside, it's a long ways to walk.

These things take their toll, the work and the toil,
It's not easy getting your living from the soil.
Her hip joints wore out, she could no longer go.
They would have to be replaced, so more calves
    she could grow.

A Dr. Davis would do it for her; this was her plan.
The very best hip doctor in New Mexico land.
She put all her trust in him, and it came out just fine.
That old hip he fixed, and it's not in a bind.

Still looking for those baby calves to show,
Out there watching them, in springtime or snow.
She is really a good rancher, being a woman or not,
Her life long partner, Andrew, sure taught her a lot.

Those Lean Years

Though my worldly possessions are meager and lean,
My life has been full and my memories are keen.
From my early beginning with Mother and Dad,
My brothers and sister have made me so glad.

Money was scarce and life could be mean,
But we had plenty to eat and always stayed clean.
A number-two washtub and a good rub board,
Mother would scrub, but the work was so hard.

There were cows to milk, and we saved the cream
To buy groceries and stuff, mostly flour and beans.
With a cotton sack dragging and new gloves to wear,
We could make enough money for new underwear.

Lace-up shoes to wear gave me no thrill,
But they would be warm and stop the chill.
New hat and boots was what I wanted most,
But when there is no money, you have to coast.

I remember our first car; it was a Model A.
You could drive twenty-five on a good highway.
A one-seater it was, with no place to hide.
The space by the back window is where I got to ride.

Mother and Daddy, with four kids in the floor,
The man we fussed at most was Henry Ford.
It beat a wagon and team though, like we had,
And twenty-five miles an hour wasn't that bad.

I look back on those lean years, and they didn't last
    that long.
A lot of miles and a lot of years, are a long time gone.
Looking back on all of the good times and all of the bad,
I would never change those lean years with Mother and Dad.

Those were the Hoover years, and in case you don't know,
The Big Depression in twenty-nine had begun to show.
There were no jobs anywhere to be had,
You worked where you could, and was mighty glad.

One dollar a day, if you could find the job,
And lucky to get it, if you could beat the mob.
Twelve hours a day, with no time to rest,
You gave them your all and your very best.

Daddy could do it; he was young and strong,
He was tough as wet leather, with muscle like stone.
It was the WPA, when there is no cotton to pull,
He loaded trucks with a shovel till they were full.

Seven miles to work is how far he walked,
His shoes were worn out; I could hear them talk.
He would lace them together with a piece of baling wire
As he sat at night by a wood-burning fire.

How those lean years still linger in my mind,
They make me know my Mother and Daddy,
    were one of a kind.
All the hardships and burdens that they had to bear
Makes me know their kind is so very rare.

There was never any cussing, or fussing, or fight,
Only warmth and friendship and love at night.
Theirs was the perfect love, you could see at a glance,
Each for the other, their lives they enhanced.

Mother is gone now, but not lost in time,
The Lord called her home at fifty-nine.
Daddy is gone also to the skies of blue,
The Lord called him to meet her at sixty-two.

No more hardships, troubles, or strife,
They fought the good fight and lived a good life.
The race here they ran like a thoroughbred,
Working and toiling just to stay ahead.

They did it in style and never gave up,
Five kids to love them I guess was enough.
That they had, and a whole lot more,
But life was sure tough, just east of Seymour.

Written in loving memory of my mother and dad

The Davis Family

Clyde (top), William, Orpha Mae (next to top), CA, Leroy, and Janis (bottom row)

The Outlaw

In days of old, when ways were bold, and Billy was
    just a kid,
The west was young, and guns were strung, around waists
    so thin and hid.
Life was cheap, and they played for keeps, as Boot Hill
    will imply,
You wore 'em low, and was never slow, or else you
    was gonna die.

Speed was the thing, or you sure might swing from a
    tree limb hanging low,
They kept them oiled, and practiced recoil, for a draw that
    wouldn't be slow.
A walk down the street, could be so fleet, when you played
    this outlaw game,
Just stay loose to avoid the noose, for the challenge
    when it came.

Billy could take a life with a gun or a knife, and never
    feel the shame,
He would throw lead, straight to the head, and give the
    other man the blame.
He was a young man once, and had no lust to kill,
    cripple or maim,
Then in a bar one night, he got in a fight with a cowboy
    gone insane.

His temper flared, from words of dare, for all to see
    and hear,
His gun was there, so he reached and drawed, he would
    show no fear.
With the speed of light, in the middle of the night, the
    cowboy lay there dead,
A forty-four bullet had found its mark right to the
    cowboy's head.

This started a life of run or fight, and the young outlaw knew
It would be a life of run and hide, with his pictures
  on review.
Lonesome and alone, and right or wrong, the good life
  was long gone,
Death would come in the afternoon sun or the early
  morning dawn.

It felt so good when he rose and stood in the misty
  morning dew,
He had become the fastest thing the West had ever knew.
But his time would come in the morning sun, his days
  on earth were few,
Too much fame at this outlaw game, as his reputation grew.

His gun was worn and his holster was torn from all
  the men he had killed,
Each passing day, he thought of a way, for a new life
  to unveil.
He was tired of the fame and this outlaw game, with his
  pictures on review,
But too many men wanted to win, so his days left on earth
  were few.

Cold blue stare or long blonde hair, his enemies were
  all the same,
A walk down the street, then plant your feet, were all
  part of the game.
Make no fuss, but speed was a must, if you wanted to
  stay alive,
Just reach low, and then let go, and leave before the
  crowd arrived.

This day was the same, as he watched the train, pull in from
  out of the West.
He checked his gun and thought about fun as he grabbed
  his coat and vest.
The train pulled in, and that was when this stranger's
  face he saw,
High cheekbones, and long keen nose, and nerves that
  seemed real raw.
A big black hat, and a long mustache, and a gun that was
  ready for the draw,

His face was mean, and his eyes were keen, with a long scar
   on his jaw.
With a second look, and the way he looked, this man was
   no outlaw,
He started to leave, and couldn't believe, the stranger said,
   "Outlaw draw."

So he reached real low for his gun to show this stranger
   who was best.
But his mistake was when he went for fun to the train from
   out of the West.
The stranger's gun really came undone as the bullet
   found its mark,
The outlaw lay dead from white, hot lead as the bullet
   found his heart.

He did not gloat as he removed his coat to cover this
   outlaw man.
There was no fun when a man's life spun in streets of
   hot white sand.
He arose to go, and that's when it showed, a silver
   shiny star.
This was his job, when men kill and rob, to find and
   stop them where they are.

Billy The Kid
Picture from *The Cattleman Magazine*, Fort Worth, Texas.

Brown Sugar

She has a lot of style; her color's all brown,
The prettiest little head that could ever be found.
So graceful and feminine, she's all class,
No amount of money could buy her, there's not
   that much cash.

Her daddy's a champion, by the great "Gay Bar King,"
Her mother has a cutting ROM; that makes her a queen.
A cutting mare deluxe, she was seldom beaten.
Just bring on the competition, the pot we will sweeten.

"Brown Sugar" we call her, 'cause that's the best kind.
You have to like this little doll, unless you are blind.
Still just a baby, she will be big some day.
Until that time comes, she can run and play.

Little tail a-flagging, and nose in the air,
Everything's a booger, and boogers beware.
We was looking for a Paint, but no color was found.
Dolores wouldn't trade her for money, not pound for pound.

Boomer Doc

Black as the night, still just a colt,
A cracker jack good one, I tell you, no joke.
Little doll head, with big round eyes,
A long big hip, with muscle on his thighs.

A nice short back made right to straddle,
With withers up front, to hold a saddle.
Thin little throatlatch on a long keen neck,
You know before long he will get you a paycheck.

His daddy is the best, being "Gay Doc's Spot."
In front of a cow, he's always red hot.
His mother is good also, "Miss Country Pine."
When having good babies, she knows the signs.

Still just a baby, so we will wait and see.
Will he be a champion? How good will he be?
We will help him grow with care and good feed.
I wager my paycheck, this colt will succeed!

Rough String Rider

Bring 'em in boys, cause I've got work to do.
I'm the rough string rider, for the ole Flying U.
As they come through the gate, I give out a squall.
There's duns, grays, and roans, and a couple of pie-balds.

They are all fours and fives and never felt a human hand.
That bronc pen over there is where we will begin.
I pick up my catch rope and follow them in,
The boys are all watching, to see who will win.

As they circle around me, all scared, wild, and fleet,
I decide on the roan, and pick up both front feet.
He hits the ground hard, then gets up like a flash.
But I've already snubbed him; he can't shed my grass.

The hackamore goes on first, then I cinch on my wood,
Cheek him and step on, right where he stood.
As he looks up and sees me, all hell breaks loose.
His one aim is to throw me, then to vamoose.

But I know my job and can sure earn my pay.
I can't let him throw me. What would the boys say?
I've got him rode good as he runs out of wind.
His life as a cow horse is about to begin.

February 1, 1990

Time Change

The world we live in today, the year of eighty-nine,
Is not like it was long ago when everything was fine.
There was so little crime, and you never heard of dope.
The strongest thing they knew about was aspirin or Coke.

Sex crimes today, are all over the news.
Turn the radio or TV on if you want to get the blues.
It's a D.W.I., rape, or a policeman got killed,
An official stole a lot of money and received a no bill.

A TV preacher got rich off the needy and the poor.
It's not supposed to be like that, we know for sure.
The preachers worked like everyone else, and did their best,
Then preached God's word to everyone when they
    stopped to rest.

They never judged a man by his many years in school,
And everyone tried to live right by the Golden Rule.
You gave your word and that was always enough.
There wasn't many lawyers, cause their life was real rough.

Long ago it was the weather, the talk of the day,
Now it's sex and violence, and what the gays have to say.
They talk it and flaunt it with no shame or remorse.
Not even Billy Graham could get them on course.

It seems our presidents have lost their leading ways,
Not anything like old George or Honest Abe.
It's a hostage, or Contra, or old Panama.
We just watch and wait, until we've lost it all.

This country's strength always came from the home.
Dad set the standards and the home was Mom's throne.
A little fuss now and to the divorce court they go,
No matter how many kids they need to watch grow.

Get that child support and make him pay and pay.
Before he gets through, he'll be old and gray.
It has become a way of life, and the profits are plenty,
Throwing those kids around like they were so much confetti.

They married one time, and that was always for life.
Somehow they made it last forever, no matter the strife.
Now it's all over cause "I don't love you anymore,"
Or "I just don't want to be married, because it's a chore."

The wedding vows they take is a laugh and a shame.
Changing partners these days has become a big game.
It's not like before, when our country was still young,
They just got married once and they never came undone.

The books we read today have no ethics or reform,
Mostly a lot of gossip, or violence, or porn.
The kind they used to read just lies there on the table,
All filled with true stories, like Cain and Abel.

Some day it will change and be like before.
The message is loud; you can hear it roar.
A big earthquake out West, or a hurricane.
If people can't read that message, they are insane.

It was once love and respect, and what will people think?
Now it's, "I don't care, if I want to, I'll drink."
Our lives touch everyone, one way or another,
Not just a few, like Mother or Brother.

Now life is still good, and it's not all bad.
There are always those grandkids to make you glad.
Let's give them some roots and a firm foundation,
So when they get where we are, they will have a great nation!

October 25, 1989

47

Poco San Bueno

Big Poco is what we called you, and it fit so well.
I never stepped on you that my head didn't swell.
So big, the look of eagles in your eye.
Anyone who ever rode you was one lucky guy.

Never any trouble is the way I remember you,
So easy to train, never a problem to shoe.
A big stout Paint stallion, colored so fine,
Always a marvel, the way you would shine.

I remember the first show, in old Abilene.
Dolores on the lead shank, you made her a queen.
A big open class it was, but that bothered you none,
When the judges were through, you were the one.

That was your first, but it was not your last.
Just working and being around you made my life a blast.
I remember old Forth Worth, when we made the Futurity,
A three-year-old you were, not near to maturity.

You worked really well, everyone was real proud.
When your run was over, that arena looked plowed.
My friend, Mr. Joe, watched you keep that cow on course.
He remarked, "That you was sure pretty good for
    a Pevehouse horse."

I would bring you back, if only I could.
I would love to brush you, then cinch on my wood.
Just one more time in front of a cow,
Dodging and turning and showing them how.

I loved your big hips, the flow of your tail,
The way you could travel, down an old cow trail.
Such a dear friend, that gentle giant,
Why did you have to leave us that dark, sad night?

We will meet again sometime, my old friend.
Right now I can't say just exactly when.
Up there in horse heaven, you will still be the king,
With your mane and tail flowing, your color so clean.

The cowboys will marvel at such a pretty sight.
They have love for a stallion who doesn't paw, kick, or bite.
There is some old cuttin' horse trainers up there for sure.
Will you ever give them a ride on that heavenly floor?

My friend, Mr. Joe, will watch you again put on your show,
That old cow trying, but by you she won't blow.
This way and that way, to keep her on course.
Mr. Joe will say, "That's sure pretty good for
    a Pevehouse horse."

Real Cowboy

"What makes a real cowboy?" my friend wanted to know.
"Does he wear a badge so his profession will show?"
In a way he does, I answers with a smile.
If you know what to look for, you can tell him a mile.

My friend's question was hard, but the answers are plenty.
Real cowboys I've known number maybe fifteen or twenty.
They are few and far between, but they are still out there.
You can't tell by a hat or boots that they wear.

Look at his hands, there should be a few calluses.
You don't get these, on the streets of old Dallas.
Will he look you in the eye while having a talk?
Is he kinda bow legged or stiff when he walks?

His years have been spent looking after range cattle.
Miles have been traveled from the seat of a saddle.
He's had plenty of time to know what's right or wrong,
To whittle on a wood chip or hum an old song.

Kinfolks and good friends are dear to his heart.
When talking to him, he is never coy or smart.
He is honest and loyal, beyond any question.
Should help be needed, he is first with the suggestion.

His skin might be brown, or look like old leather,
From a lifetime spent horseback in all kinds of weather.
Good times and bad times, heartache and pain,
He's seen them all, but he's still the same.

Never a big talker, about all he has done,
Just minds his own business, working from sun to sun.
Gossip and small talk has never been his style.
He has better things to talk about, more worthwhile.

His look became all puzzled, from the answers I gave him.
A real cowboy is not always all tall, lean, and trim.
You will never know from one look or a glance,
He didn't get to be a real cowboy just by chance.

To really get to know one may take you awhile,
Though he may look all common, you will find he has style.
His living standards are a thrill and a joy.
This is what really makes him, A REAL COWBOY!

June 13, 1991

Gem Crow

"Crow" was a big gray horse of the Appaloosa breed.
Just another horse, for someone to feed.
That's what they all thought, until they gave him a try,
Ole Crow could do it all; the limit was the sky.

Now with a name like "Crow," he had a lot to live down.
Every performance to him was dead serious; he was
    never a clown.
When Crow's name was announced, the crowd would get
    real quiet,
He would be running to win, be it daytime or night.

Chester Sanchez wanted to retire "Crow" at the age of eighteen.
Little Tonia wanted "Crow" and he would make her a queen.
She had his confidence; the little girl could do it all.
High point every year she rode him, they were having a ball.

Tonia started riding "Crow" when only eight, or maybe nine.
He was so faithful and never got her in a bind.
The pole-bending game was what he liked the best.
Set 'em up any way, north, south, east, or west.

Turn his back to the poles, then wait for the grunt,
Then turn and ride good, cause "Crow" was on the hunt.
This he did so well, they have him an ROM.
Now everyone knew why his first name was "Gem."

"Crow" was born coal black, no color could be found.
His owner looked at him in wonder and then kicked the ground.
When he reached two, the color was white as snow.
Big black spots on the hips sure gave him a glow.

Little Tonia had done so well year after year,
Her dad S.J. wanted to try it, if he could find the right gear.
Already forty-seven, so he started kinda late.
Being a winner on "Crow" wasn't always fate.

Steer dobbing, bareback equitation, S.J. did quite well.
All the things he did on "Crow could make a head swell.
Seventy-three years between them, Gem Crow and S.J.
Having fun like two kids seemed to make their day.

Gem Crow is gone now; he left us at twenty-six,
No more to run the barrels or bend the sticks.
Always dear to our hearts, the memories are there to stay.
They will give a world of happiness when our skies seem gray.

Crow is gone now, but he will always have love.
We know he flew to heaven, just like a dove.
He is running the poles again where you never grow old,
And remembering the good times that have never been told.

Written for my good friends
S.J. and Kay Bryan
December 22, 1990

Old Zapata

A small border town, for a thousand years or more,
Gone forever, it's now just a Falcon Lake Shore.
The people who lived there all those many years ago
Can never return there to watch their family grow.

It's now just a lake of water, on the world globe,
What used to be people living in houses of adobe.
They moved everything there, even the graves,
The water devoured that town as if it were a cave.

Seems like everything has to get older before it can
    get good,
The new town they would go, but they would stay here
    if they could.
"Making way for progress," is what they were told.
No time to be sentimental for their ways of old.

Zapata is where they brought Poncho Villa, across
    the saddle, one day,
The soldiers had killed him, how no one would say.
He took from the wealthy and gave to the poor.
Their champion was dead, he could help them no more.

The peasants refused to believe he was dead and gone.
They needed him to lead them and help right the wrong.
The soldiers brought him to the gazebo, where speeches
    are made,
And threw him from the saddle, and then rode away.

Lake water now covers that historical spot,
Given up for progress, they sure gave a lot.
But there's no time to be sentimental, we have celebrating
    to do.
We will have this last big rodeo, but it must be on cue.

One big celebration, and it was to be their last.
With the town half moved, they would have to be fast.
A big "Buck Out" Rodeo was what they would have.
I was there folks, and I can see it all now.

Quick put together chutes made out of yellow pine.
Big, bad Brahma bulls that could roar like a lion.
I rode one of those that day, just to help with the show,
And won the bull riding at their last big rodeo.

Wild, bad, bucking horses that looked like mustangs,
There was sure no Doc Bars or Pocos in this outlaw string.
They were flea-bitten grays, and some vinegar roans,
All with little pig eyes and a big roman nose.

The year was the early fifties, as I recall,
And I think about it often as I stare at the wall.
I would love to go back there, just to see that place,
But I know I can't do that, too much water to face.

What a rodeo it was, and it lasted two days,
Something to be remembered, for the past when they gazed.
Just almost over, where they had lived for so long,
To look back with bitterness to them would be wrong.

Sourdough

Sourdough was with us, but he had to go away,
And as I think about him, there are many things to say.
He passed on the other day at the age of twenty-four,
Such a good and loyal servant for two decades and more.

Sourdough's what we called him, but it could have been
    "the big gray."
If you had a tough job for him, he would always find a way.
You could work him all day, in hard land or sand.
When the gather was made, he would sure make you a hand.

He knew how to work cows, and he did it so well.
When dragging calves to the fire, he'd make your
    head swell.
He could get you right up there, then drag them right out,
And didn't want you missing, or fooling about.

Work was all business to him, and he sure knew how.
Sourdough could get down on a cow, or catch it right now.
When you needed to load anything, big or small, it was
    all the same.
Just get your grass on it; old Sourdough was game.

Now he wasn't a halter horse in your wildest imagination,
But he was a real cowboy's horse, not some imitation.
A big stout gray horse, about fifteen two or three,
And had the prettiest way of going that you will ever see.

Just take him to town, if you wanted to rope steers.
He taught two boys real well, by the name of Locklar.
Sourdough was their first teacher several years ago,
And contributed so very much just to help them both grow.

To prove he was an all around, and could do about anything,
Debbie Locklar ran the cloverleaf on him; he sure liked
    that game.
There was one other thing he did, and I will tell it to you,
All the horses that have done this are far between and few.

There was this horseback wedding these folks wanted
    to have.
Sourdough was there, just to kinda show them how.
He carried the groom that day, who was all aglow,
And kept everything in line, so there was no big rodeo.

Now if horses have a heaven, and I'm real sure they do,
Sourdough is belly deep in grass, and the water is pure blue.
Angels are riding him, with saddles of pure gold,
He is sleek and pretty up there where you never grow old.

November 17, 1989

Thankful at Thanksgiving

Thankful for the blessings
      I have received in this
life.
For the arm that was
   around me
      During troubles and
strife.

Thankful for my parents,
Who helped me to grow.
For my mother's love,
And the way it could glow.

Thankful to my dad
For never being mean,
And teaching me to go on
When life would get lean.

Thankful for a home,
And a dear loving wife.
For her understanding,
And sharing my life.

Thankful for the friends
I've had along the way.
Bless and keep them
For all of their days.

Thankful for the food
You give me to eat.
For a nice warm bed
At night while I sleep.

Thankful for the weather,
In winter time or spring.
For not hearing
   my complaints
About snowfall or rain.

Thankful for your
   forgiveness
When I would do wrong.
For showing only love
When reprimands belong.

November 22, 1989

Sad, Happy, Christmas

Christmas time is here again.
What does it mean to you?
Happy, loving, joyous times,
Sometimes sad, sometimes blue.

Thinking about bygone days
With loved ones who have gone.
To think of them with sadness,
To me, does not seem wrong.

This is the day it happened
All those many years ago.
God sent the world a savior
So all mankind could glow.

On this earth but thirty-three years,
But such an impression made.
"Just love and follow me," He said.
"Your souls I sure will save."

Jesus gave all mankind hope
For a better life, later on.
He said he would be waiting
Just for us, there on his heavenly throne.

December 1989

Paint Ranch Christmas

Christmas Time again,
It's the year of eighty-nine.
The spirits here are great,
Cause our horses are fine.

Their hair is sure long,
With bellies round and big.
Just can't wait for feeding time,
They all eat like a pig.

They are eating for two.
Only time will tell
What the other one looks like,
When the babies expel.

Christmas time now.
We love it so much.
We have two a year, you know,
With the horses and such.

The other one is in the spring,
When the babies arrive.
Watching, hoping, and praying
They all will survive.

Hoping they will have color,
Whether they are male or female.
The surprise will have to wait
    For a time called "Christmas Corral."

December 2, 1989

60

Old Mare

I'm just an old broodmare, all thin and old.
My one great joy was when my babies would foal.
I've lived in great pastures, where the grazing was good,
And little stomp pens, where you would leave if you could.

A rodeo performer when I was young and fleet,
I always made 'em look good; they double-hocked both feet.
It was fun and a thrill to run on fresh-plowed soil,
Then put your hocks in the ground when that rope uncoiled.

The lights and the crowd and the music would play,
A top cowboy was up there like he meant to stay.
We won the calf roping that day, the dogging too.
I can still hear him whisper, "It's just me and you."

Those were the good times and I wish for them still.
I can still hear the crowd and remember the thrill.
The admiring looks they gave me, the pat of a hand,
Just being a winner can sure 'nuff be grand.

My good looks are gone now and I'm old and gray.
So many babies have made my back sway.
This pasture is long gone, cause the rain didn't come.
My ribs are showing and my joints hurt some.

They don't bother me any more; I'm just left here alone.
I'm down on my luck, just a bag of bone.
The next time you see me, I could be in a store,
Or in front of some poodle on somebody's floor.

I know this life here can't be everlasting,
But I sure hate to be some poodle's Ken-L-Ration!

June 10, 1991

Let's Rodeo

What has happened to the Rodeo at our Lea County Fair?
They used to be really great, and done with a flair.
Rank stock and good cowboys can be a wonder and
    a marvel,
But we've let our good rodeo turn into a carnival.

What ever happened to Coloman, Butler Brothers, or Stiner?
They make the Lea Production look like a one-liner.
What happened to ole Tuffy Cooper, the best of the best?
He could call a rodeo the way it was, a way out West.

Cowboys are not rock and rollers, as some seem to think.
The tradition they live by makes the dirty jokes stink.
With more world champions in Lea County, gives
    plenty to brag,
But the way our rodeo is being presented is really a drag.

When the band starts playing some silly rock and roll,
Your mind wonders back to those days of old.
It was COUNTRY WESTERN, done Cowboy style,
Songs done by Hank, or Lefty, or Earnest, like
    "I'd Walk a Mile."

I remember all the great cowboys, and so good they were,
Oliver with a rope, and how Shoulders and Tibbs could spur.
In their time they were the best, but we still have some now
That could give them some lessons and still show them how.

The National Finals in '88, and it had never been done,
Jim Sharp won the bull riding; he rode every one.
Voted "Rookie of the Year" in '87, and
    that was a lot,
He is the very best on bad and rank stock.

When you compare great ropers and all they have done,
Your mind goes to Roy Cooper, and he is the one.
Eight times he won the World against the very best,
Not counting the two they stole lays them all to rest.

Just when they thought there was no more from that
   great mold,
Along comes cousin Jimmie Cooper, and new
   records unfold.
All-around cowboy, and into the Hall Of Fame,
With a rope and fast horse: Rodeo is his game.

These are just a few great cowboys I've admired for so long.
The great cowboys are still here, they are not all gone.
It's up to the old cowboys to keep it like it was,
Wild, simple, and western, like when the West was won.

We don't need a lot of ballyhoo on a microphone
From a rodeo announcer, who makes a chair his throne.
Let's get it back right, and do it western style,
So all the old cowboys can watch and smile!!!

The Paint Mare Priss

A good-looking mare, she is by "The Saint."
Cross her with "Profit" and hope for a Paint.
Watching and waiting the whole year through,
This one will be different, maybe red, white & blue.

Priss will do it just for us,
A loud filly or colt, but color's a must.
We raised Priss with love, sometimes even a kiss.
Real special to our hearts, there's only one Priss.

Ole Profit is a Quarter, so color is a gamble.
If this baby's not Paint, I may have to ramble.
Moaning and groaning, foaling time has come.
I feel the need of a beer or a bottle of rum.

So excited from watching and waiting so long,
Please let this one come straight, don't let it be wrong.
It's coming now, we can see the bubble.
Just be quiet and wait in case she's in trouble.

The feet come first, they sure look black to me.
Hoping for a Paint, but we'll have to wait and see.
There's its head, but wait, this is taking too long.
We will have to help her, so try to be strong.

Time is passing too fast, pull hard and true.
There she is, we've got her, this job is through.
Look around here Priss and see what you have done,
A loud-colored Paint filly, she's a son-of-a-gun.

We will name her good, just any name won't do.
She'll have it for life, so let's get it on cue.
After much thought for a month or so,
We chose a name that will make her glow.

"Calico Party Doll," that will be her name.
She will carry it to fortunes, glory, and fame.
Old Abilene town is where she will begin.
The tough weanling futurity is what she will win.

One year later, and wouldn't you know,
She won the yearling Futurity at that big show.
From Abilene to El Paso, and all in between,
When they line 'em up at halter, she's the queen.

From halter to performance was no surprise.
She's a beautiful painted lady with no disguise.
"Thanks" go to Priss for giving us this thrill.
All the joy she has given us, would give you a chill.

You were bred by Elmer Nash, who is not with us now,
But long to be remembered, through you somehow.
We will keep you and love you forever, I suppose.
Perhaps there are horses in Heaven. Who knows?

But if Priss should pass on before our last sunrise,
We will send her up there to you, Elmer. My, what
     a surprise!
She'll run and play in green pastures, from daylight to dark.
You will take real good care of her in that heavenly park.

First Love

Just a pretty country girl, with ways so simple and true,
With days filled with laughter, she was never sad or blue.
Her best dress was made of gingham, or maybe calico,
Always washed and ironed, so not a wrinkle showed.

Her hair was in pigtails, or sometimes down with a bow.
With eyes the bluest blue, strange how they would glow.
Always with a twinkle in them, for everyone to see,
What a thrill it was when she would look at me.

It took very little to make her happy, there on the farm,
A picture show sometimes, or a party out in the barn.
Dancing cotton-eyed Joe with her skirts all a-whirl,
Laughing up at everyone with teeth white as pearls.

Her mind was pure and clean as a running brook.
The natural beauty she had would fill a good-sized book.
She never knew the charm and wonder of her ways,
But the joy she spread would last for days and days.

With skill and what a thrill to touch her soft white hand,
My every thought was that some day I'd fix it with a band.
But when you are fifteen, and green, with growing up to do,
You only sit and daydream about eyes of bluest blue.

Executive Brother

A post office exec, never little or mean,
He has the best operation you've ever seen.
Born to be a leader, he is one of a kind.
His operation is the best, not the blind leading the blind.

Proud to call him my brother, always just and fair,
With his suit and tie on, he handles business with flair.
He is never too busy to have a little fun.
He does this so easy, while being on the run.

I have known him for a while, in fact all his life.
It hasn't been easy; there was trouble and strife.
But he is made of the right kind of mettle.
When the going got real tough, he was never soft or brittle.

When we were little and both on the farm,
We always had Mother and Daddy to keep us from harm.
Now that we are older and gone our own ways,
The love and teaching they gave us will last all our days.

There is no way to explain the love I have for
    this brother of mine,
Always there for me when my life was in a bind.
There is no way to repay what he has done for me.
He has always kept me going for a better life to see.

A Christian at heart and always seeks God's will,
His account is paid up there; he has no past-due bill.
I hope he lives forever and is happy with glee.
I thank him so much for always being there for me.

March 20, 1990

The Truck-Driving Man

He was the last one, of the Clyde Davis clan.
They saved the best for last. This man's a hand.
He drives an eighteen-wheeler up and down the road,
Hauling freight all over; it's a heavy load.

From Houston to Tulsa, three times a week,
He keeps it rolling, sometimes with no sleep.
A big truck jockey like you've seldom ever seen,
Always alert and do it like a pro, with his senses keen.

Now he sets real tall at the steering wheel,
If a four-wheeler wants to play, it's a "no deal."
With two hands on the wheel and his eyes on the road,
He takes care of that freight behind him; it's a heavy load.

A little wife at home, waiting for his return.
Getting back to be with her is his main concern.
As he leaves Houston, heading for old Tulsa town,
He vows to be careful, never act like a clown.

He is good at what he does, as the records will show.
A million miles he has driven on every kind of road.
He's a God-fearing Christian; I've known him all his life.
Richard knows how to handle the good times,
    along with the strife.

I'm proud to call him my brother, this truck-driving man.
Not a lazy bone in him, he can sure make a hand.
He keeps his foot on the pedal, his eyes on the highway.
That big trailer behind him never wobbles or sways.

"Back that big rig in here, this is where your load goes."
It's long and narrow. Will that big trailer go?
            He slips it in reverse and starts it on back.
Without ever a bobble, he centered the rack.

Born to be a truck driver, this brother of mine,
Put him in an office and he would be in a bind.
The open highway is what be really loves,
The dew on the trees, and the flight of the doves.

"Just keep on a trucking," that's his code and motto.
If you get tired and sleepy, just don't let it show.
Do it on pride when the going gets tough.
This brother is my hero, a diamond in the rough.

March 13, 1990

Living Your Dreams

He's got cowboy blood flowing in his veins.
If you need a horse trained, just hand him the reins.

He can pick the right calf, right out of the herd,
To think that he'll lose him is totally absurd.

He can take a good horse and teach him all the new tricks,
Makes those ole calves think they're in a heck of a fix.

This cowboy grew up working and living down on the farm,
But he always loved horses and would rather be out in the barn.

He has quite an eye for picking the right critter,
For him life on the farm just didn't have much glitter.

He spent some time at the rodeo, rode some that were
    really bad.
I'd say he did quite well, considering the time that he had.

But training good cutting horses creates his biggest joy.
When it comes to teaching cow sense, he never is coy.

I'm really quite proud of this brother of mine.
When it comes to horse sense and teaching, he sure is fine.

He led me to Christ when I was just fifteen.
To his brother it was good or bad with no in-between.

When I almost drowned, he pulled me from Haskin's big tank.
Whatever I am or become, I have this dear brother to thank.

I'm happy he's now doing what he always wanted it seems.
Life sure can be good when you're living your dreams.

He's got a sweet wife, who loves animals and horses to boot.
The one he had before her didn't seem to give a hoot.

Doing extra good at a show or cutting just busts his shirt
   at the seams,
Yes, life sure can be sweet when two people are
   living their dreams.

Written by my brother
C. A. Davis
March 31, 1990

Heartfelt Years

This is the story of five siblings: The Clyde and Orpha
   Davis clan,
It's not meant to be funny, just fit into God's great plan.
Three were born in the Depression to Orpha and Clyde.
When poverty came looking, there was nowhere to hide.

One was born a little later, the other during World War Two.
Five hungry mouths to feed, man that's quite a few.
We all grew up just fine and healthy as should be.
We didn't mind being poor, cause we were all happy
   you see.

There weren't many trips to church, we'll tell you right
   out loud.
The right clothes were not available, and Mom was
   too proud.
For our Sunday school lesson, Mom and Dad lived the
   good life.
We had homegrown Christianity that would withstand
   life's strife.

They taught us to value God, Country, Family, and Friends,
And especially trust in the Lord upon whom all depends.
Many years since our upbringing have gone by the board.
Our sweet Mother and Daddy are now with the Lord.

Now four of five siblings are getting on in years.
We look back on our happy childhood and fight back
   the tears.
The youngest brother is now middle-aged.
Our lives were so blessed, it's as though they were staged.

We look back in wonder of all that has transpired.
When thinking of our childhood, we never grow tired.
God must have loved Clyde and Orpha, to make us all
   so free,
Just to love one another and try like Him to be.

The family has all scattered with families of their own.
Still, our minds often go back to that sweet place
    called home.
We see each other less often now; the miles are too far.
We still feel the love for each other wherever we are.

When our lives are all over and we're nothing but clay,
In the presence of God, together forever, oh what a great day!
With our loved ones departed, the beauty to behold,
Four brothers and a sister will walk on streets of pure gold.

C. A. Davis
March 30, 1990

Dedicated by C. A. Davis to his sister, Janis Horton and three brothers, William, Leroy, and Richard Davis.

Janis Laverne Davis Horton

The only girl, in a family of five kids,
You was the weaker sex, but for so long you kept it hid.
In the cotton patch, with three rows between us,
Pull that outside row, then get the middle one or bust.

You beat me often, the first ever to pull
   five hundred pounds,
But I never heard you gloat, or make me a clown.
The work had to be harder, you being a girl and all,
But I never heard you complain, always there, fall for fall.

Then came our schooling, or what little we had.
The cotton was all pulled; this made us all glad.
Always the smartest, you could breeze right through,
Trying to keep up, for me, was a time to be blue.

You always helped me, was never smart aleck or coy.
What I liked about you most then, you was one of the boys.
As I look back now, there's one thing I know,
You was always a lady, I know this, as older I grow.

Blessed forever to have a sister like you,
You always added happiness and made my skies pure blue.
My greatest inspiration, you made me want to win.
So lucky the Good Lord wanted me to be your twin.

Those first years I cherish, as I remember me and you,
Working, playing together, it was always me and you.
I would never change the way it was back then for us.
There was only love, never bickering or fuss.

The years we had together numbered eighteen,
Together from the beginning, no separation in between.
As we grew older, our life's path had to part,
But I have always kept you in the corner of my heart.

So very dear to me, always so understanding.
My life sometimes a-drift, you always helped with
   my landing.
Mistakes we both made, seems like they were plenty.
Heartaches we've both had, seems a way too many.

God loved us, I guess. He put our lives back on course.
With you, it's the love of your family, with me it's a horse.
With you, it's your church work, and the people you know.
With me, it's my dear wife, and getting horses ready
   to show.

No more cotton to pull and breaking our back.
Sometimes I look behind me and can still see that sack.
The good thing I remember, when I look "a way back then,"
Is growing up and being with my wonderful TWIN.

April 12, 1990

Clyde William Davis

The oldest of five, the first to come along,
In my mother's eyes the best, you could do no wrong.
It took all these years for me to see
What she knew all along, the best you would be.

We grew up together, back there on the farm.
You kinda looked after me and kept me from harm.
Things that happened then I have never forgotten.
Some things fell your way, that was kind of rotten.

We all had to work hard from daylight till dark.
There was no time to play, or visit the park.
If there was cotton to pull, that's where we would be,
There before daylight and as long as we could see.

You being the oldest, you always emptied the sacks.
I never heard you complain about your sore aching back.
If Grandpa was with us, you emptied his also.
Such a respectful grandson our mother did grow.

The time at the golf course, all happy, eager, and green,
We met these tough city boys, all bigger and mean.
We had gone there to caddy, for money and the fun.
They started cussing at us and you said, "Leroy, run."

I can't remember being so scared, before or since.
Nothing could have stopped me, not horses or fence.
I left there a-flying, and I was right on your heels.
That was the first I remember fear, I know how it feels.

The scar on your nose I remember so well.
You fell from a cotton wagon while finishing a bale.
The cut was real bad, with blood everywhere.
I looked at you with eyes beginning to blur.

But big kids don't cry, so I walked away.
You never knew the love I had for you that day.
Life hasn't been easy, as we both well know.
But somehow we survived, and managed to grow.

Really quite different, being full brothers and all.
With me it was horses, with you it was cars I recall.
They told it so often, your first words was "ace the car."
You could identify every one, from near or afar.

You learned to drive at a very early age.
Your chin was about level with the wheel and the gauge.
Many years have passed since those happy times.
Now you are truck driver, running all kinds of lines.

One of the best at driving a big rigged-up truck.
You do it with skill and never leave it to luck.
I can picture you now, as you go down the road,
Carefree and happy, pulling all kinds of loads.

You have worked everywhere, cleaning up other
    people's mess.
The first town job you had was the old S & S.
The next one I remember may ring a bell,
It was stocking and carrying out at the old L & L.

Then it was the oil field, somewhere in between.
Climbing that derrick to make a trip can sure be mean.
Ice everywhere, the floor slick, cold and wet.
You did it like a champion, you haven't given up yet.

Then your big break came, it was long overdue,
Your first truck-driving job, and I'll give them a clue.
They made no mistake when they hired this boy from
    the farm.
You did it with style and laid on the charm.

You've hauled about everything, including a corpse.
This kept you wide-awake, as you kept it on course.
Then it was Dallas, a supervisor you became,
A farm boy in the city, but it was all the same.

You had what it takes, to walk life's treadmill.
I marveled at your courage, and it stays with me still.
What's in the future, none of us really knows.
But you sure will handle it, because your breeding shows.

Another thing I remember, that was all new to me,
The night you accepted Jesus as your savior to be.
You was so happy and all aglow.
Now I understand why, as older I grow.

So glad to be your brother and I have always been.
The memories I have of you go way back when.
I have never said "I love you" very often, I recall.
But if I had not known you, I would have missed it all.

April 3, 1990

Betty Gayle

She was ours for a little while.
But now she has gone
To be with the Master,
And share his Great Throne.

No more suffering and no more pain.
The legacy she left is our great gain.
God loved her so much as her trophies will show.
He just gave her to us a little while to help us grow.

Her spirit and her will forever come from above.
That was God's way to show us His Great Love.
Just keep her God up there in that heavenly place.
We pray to be with her again when we finish life's race.

We will all be together again sooner than we think.
We are told it can happen sooner than a blink.

With her pig tails a-flying,
And that wonderful smile.
What a joy for us all to walk
That last long mile.

Our entry fee was paid on that old Rugged Cross.
Christ did it with love so we would not all be lost.

Heaven Bound

Ticket Paid for by Jesus Christ

This man I loved for what seems such a short while
Departed the world forever. He walked his last mile.
Such a humble, kind, and gracious man,
His presence will always be remembered in this land.

Never a lot of worldly good, to brag and show,
But his smile, his laugh, and love did glow.
A heart filled with love for family and everyone.
He also loved that little truck with the rack, how it run.

Always a worker, sick or well, to keep his family fed,
Mile after mile, in that little truck, when he should have
    been in bed.
A heart condition, a diabetic also, to complicate his life.
He could not take his insulin and drive, this added to
    the strife.

This was his livelihood, the thing that he did best,
No time to lie around for the much needed rest.
He ran a good race here on this life's treadmill.
Looking back on his life gives me such a thrill.

A born-again Christian since about age fifteen,
He made that stand for Jesus, forever. His slate was clean.
Jesus died on that piece of wood for his sins and mine.
All he ever asked was that we believe, not reject, or recline.

The Holy Bible says it all in John, Chapter Three,
    Verse Sixteen,
Repent, believe in me, and you shall see the King.
William believed in Jesus Christ, he stood and made
    the walk.
I saw it with my own eyes; it's not hearsay or talk.

His name was written in the book of life not long ago.
Up there with the Lord right now, all happy and aglow.
I can see his smile, hear the sweet way he would talk,
See the back of his head, and that beautiful humble walk.

I loved this man, my brother, while he was here on earth.
Just knowing he is in Heaven sure does ease the hurt.
We will be together again; it sure won't be that long,
Up there with our Savior, with love so true and strong.

He made mistakes while here on earth, just as you and I.
Those mistakes were all forgiven; the Holy Bible
    does not lie.
God bless my brother up there in that wonderful place.
The thrill in knowing when I depart, I will see that
    beautiful face.

Written in loving memory of Clyde William Davis
February 11, 1995

My Son Bob

We named him Bobby Wayne, after a friend or two,
But after he became older, that just wouldn't do.
He shortened it a little, but Bob's still the same.
To live and serve God seemed to be his one aim.

Always a good worker, the best at most any job,
Just of the many good traits about my son Bob.
A man of few words, kinda slow when he talks,
But when Bob tells you something, you can take it and walk.

Never a boaster or bragger, about all he has done,
About the folks he has touched, or the souls he has won.
When good men are gone, this one's a little better,
Always doing God's will down to the last letter.

Touched by that great hand at such an early year,
To walk the straight and narrow, to never show fear.
He takes all life has to offer and stands like a giant,
With a smile on his face, be it day or night.

Life to him is so good because he has found the way,
He stands on firm ground, not quicksand or clay.
Destined to serve God anyway he can,
To love and to honor that nail-scarred hand.

This is a calling of love which few men will ever get.
His treasures will be in Heaven, that's no gamble or bet.
This world we live in, all wicked and forlorn,
Makes the un-believers wonder why they were born.

We all need someone to stand and point the way,
To tell us about Heaven and the great Judgment Day.
About that Great Mansion up there in the sky,
How we can all get there, and not wonder why.

Someone to tell us about old John, Peter, and Paul,
About how we can be with them, and avoid the fall.
Someone to tell us about the Bible, like John three: sixteen,
How we can live the good life, never be little or mean.

God has chosen someone to do all of these things,
That we might live the good life and know the
    happiness it brings.
He stands with the good and towers like a beacon.
No matter life's hardships, Bob will never weaken.

I contributed so very little to help this man grow.
God took over where I failed; the perfection does show.
The crime is all mine, though I didn't kill, steal, or rob.
The brightest light in my life is my son Bob.

January 14, 1991

Becky

I love that name, because it's just for you.
We picked it from many, maybe a hundred or two.
It fits you so well, as I know we did fine.
You have brought so much joy, always walked the line.
Never a problem to anyone, a pleasure and joy to me.
It started long ago, when you sat on my knee.
I have thought about your name, and I finally
   have it analyzed,
As I think about it, this is what I realize.
The "B" is for beauty and brilliance, because that is how
   I see you.
Also you were never biased or belligerent; the "B" sure
   does fit you.
The "E" is for education, that you have a lot.
Your determination was not to let your mind rot.
A degree from Texas Tech in the very highest form,
A perfect 4.0 for four years, blew them away like a storm.
The "C" is for character, and this makes you first-class,
It makes me know that my Becky's a lass.
The "K" is for kindness, and you have shown me so much,
Always so loving, never critical and such.
"Y" is for youth, and always will be to me,
No matter your age or how many tomorrows you see.

You will always have my love, if in Lubbock or old Spring.
I'll always think about you, whether horseback or in
   the swing.

Joey

"Little Joey" is my grandson.
He makes me so proud.
Just a real little cowboy,
Never noisy or loud.

He rides a bicycle
And handles it like a horse.
The front yard is his pasture.
He keeps the Shredron Ranch on course.

Really quite a good rider,
Getting places in a jiff.
He seldom gets thrown,
But sometimes he will biff.

Smart beyond his years,
This is not just idle talk.
I have known him for a while,
Even before he could walk.

Proud to be his grandpa,
Is all that I can say.
This boy is sure a good one,
And will be a great man some day.

January 9, 1990

My Friend

This story is about a man that I call my friend,
But much more to so many, is where my story will begin.
Born in hard time, with a will to excel,
He was determined to be a winner: almost compelled.

When he was just a lad, he wondered what he could do
To be success in life and right on cue.
The cowboy blood was there, flowing in his veins.
He remembered all the great cowboys; he could call them all
    by name.

The decision was made, so he would take a stand.
Few people ever saw him without a rope in his hand.
When he was in school, really a great athlete,
Playing football, baseball, or basketball, always on his feet.

These were his school years; he excelled in every course.
But there was no one who could beat him with a rope
    and a horse.
With the build of an athlete, all muscle, tall, and lean,
His trademark was a smile, the broadest ever seen.

He beat all the great ropers as his reputation grew,
Oliver, Holliman, Teague, Young, Sewalt, and Fort,
    to name a few.
A really great roper, with style so neat,
He rode some great horses, all savvy and fleet.

Never a boaster, about what he has done,
About the people he has helped, or the money he has won.
In his day he beat them all, somewhere or another.
He always stayed the same, treated friends like a brother.

To sum my friend up, so people will know,
He has always been the best friend of rodeo.
So unselfish, he shared his great talent with all,
His reward finally came just this fall.

Shrined in the Hall of Fame, in the county of Lea,
Right there with all the greats, for all future cowboys to see.
Glad to call him my friend, father of the great Super Looper,
I am telling you about no other than Dale "Tuffy" Cooper.

December 1, 1992

Cowboy of the Past

You could tell he was a cowboy
By the bow-legged way he walked.
And you knew that he was real
By what he said and how he talked.

It was plain that he was happy
With the cowboy life he had,
And the past would be remembered
By more pleasant times than bad.

Once he traveled in the fast lane,
And he loved the ladies, too.
Won and lost at playing poker,
Like most all cowboys do.

But his cowboy days are over.
Time and age have taken 'hold.
And the good times in his memory
Make it easier growing old.

Now, instead of chasing cattle,
Riding hard to bring them in,
He sits around drinking coffee,
And telling stories with his friends.

And he knows his days are numbered,
That this life will soon be gone,
And he hopes that his amigos,
Who have already gone on —

Will be "Up There" waiting for him,
With their horses ready to go.
In a place called "Cowboy Heaven,"
Which they learned of here below.

Mistakes he made along the way,
But he always took the blame.
And if he had another chance,
He'd relive it all the same.

Written by my friend
Tuffy Cooper
October 24, 1989

89

My Uncle Otis

He was left the head of the family, just barely sixteen.
This was during the Depression, life sure was mean.
A mother and sister to care for, it was on his back.
Dig a living out with a shovel, or a cotton sack.

He had to grow up fast; there were no fun years.
The head of the house, he had to quiet their fears.
Never a girlfriend to date like most boys do.
A mother and sister to care for, but he would see it through.

Not even a car to drive. When he had to get around,
He would walk or drive the mules. He was duty bound.
The mules liked to run, this was their best trick,
To the west field they would go, let 'em hit their best lick.

Standing in a flat-bed wagon, with a line in each hand,
The way he could circle those mules was simply grand.
When they had their run out, it was over that day,
Back to the house for Sister and Mother, there was
    no time for play.

Groceries to buy: mostly potatoes, flour, and beans.
A work shirt or pants: khaki or denim jeans.
Striped overalls and maybe a pair of cheap shoes,
Just the bare essentials, you couldn't pick or choose.

He grew up fast there on the Baylor County farm,
Taking care of Mother and Sister, keeping them from harm.
The chores were all his, milking, farming, and such.
To forget what he did for me is too much.

I remember the way he was, the way he could laugh.
Hard times never got him down, not even half.
He had a sense of humor, I think the very best.
When I look back now, I know he was blessed.

The Lord sent him here for all of us to love,
Sent him down here from Heaven above.
He lived the good life and it always showed.
A smile for everyone, his personality glowed.

This was a Christian; he didn't argue or fuss.
All the years I knew him, I never heard him cuss.
Just a very rare man, to be fair and live right was a must.
He ran life's race with dignity, honor, and trust.

There were bad times, when his mother passed away,
But hard times made him tough, his standards never swayed.
Nothing stays the same, not even hard times.
He lived to see it through on nickels and dimes.

He met this lady who was so beautiful and fair,
She had a face like an angel, with coal-black hair.
They fell in love and were married before too long.
Good things do happen to people who never do wrong.

My Little Grandson

My little grandson, I love him so very much.
Wise beyond his years about family and such.
A victim of a broken home, as I recall,
He had to tell his dad goodbye today; we all bawled.

His little heart was breaking as that plane took air.
Their first meeting in a year can't be fair.
A little mind doesn't understand the squabble and fuss,
Doesn't know why everyone can't just be us.

His little heart really loves both sides, you see,
And doesn't understand why with both parents he can't be.
Torn apart by jealousy, get even, and hate,
To a little six year-old this can't be fate.

It's up to everyone to make his life a little better,
We need to read the Good Book down to the last letter.
Where it says what will happen should we mistreat
   His little ones,
To me this is as plain as the morning sun.

No one can change what is or what has been.
To imagine it different would be foolhardy and sin.
His daddy loves him and will not be left out.
No one can ever change this or turn it about.

Let's just remember a little guy who has trouble,
Be a little more forgiving, cause a little less squabble.
He has plenty of love for all, I suppose.
If he has the chance, that will blossom like a rose.

"No you can't see your dad, because it's too late,"
Or, "We will be out of town," just don't rate.
You can make any excuse, to a six-year-old,
Make him believe stories that should never be told.

He will grow up some day and be very wise.
Maybe he will wonder why there was no compromise.
I, as his Grandpa, intend to stand fast,
And I'll be right here to tell him of his past.

I will tell him like it was, "You have to be home by six."
Or, "No you can't have him today. I don't have
    his clothes fixed."
This can't be very important after a wait of a year.
Too bad everyone couldn't see the heartbreak and tears.

My heart breaks for him, so what should I do?
People are like they are. I can't be you.
We could turn it all around and just call it fate.
Let him grow up with love, and never know hate.

July 10, 1991

Kristin

The picture on the TV is looking back at me,
The most beautiful little girl that you will ever see.
Little black patent shoes and white socks a pair,
Little angel face, with long, dark, soft, curled hair.

The pride of her grandparents, she gives us plenty to brag.
Always an upbeat when our life becomes a drag.
Quite a little celebrity, a child model at three,
A star on "Father Dowling," we saw it on TV.

Just a sweet little girl, who doesn't know how special she is.
Her grandparents are so proud; this granddaughter's theirs.
She acts all grown up, and never like a baby.
Kristin is just perfect and always the perfect lady.

Yes, that picture is still there for me to see when I want to.
It keeps everything real happy and our skies clear blue.
Our first grandchild, and what a joy she has been,
The sweetest little girl since the world began.

January 27, 1990

Erica

Though you were not the first, you have sure took a stand.
With your sweet little ways, you are completely grand.
A joy to everyone, you are never very much trouble.
When you came into our lives, the happiness was double.

Dogs and cats and chickens and such are your fascination.
What a joy it is, when you're around, to see
   your concentration.
Here and there and everywhere, there's just too much to see.
Life to you is a happy thing, what a joy to see your glee.

A lot like your daddy, I think, and your mother also,
The combination of them both is what makes you glow.
Big brown eyes, with a doll-like face, make you look
   just right.
Long brown hair, with skin so fair, what a beautiful sight.

We are your proud grandparents, we love you like no other.
For all the joy you bring us, we thank your dad and mother.
A sweet little lady now, though you are only four.
All grown up and great some day, your grandparents
   will keep the score.

February 3, 1990

Jennifer

What a pretty name for just the right little girl.
Beautiful doll-like face; brown hair all a-curl.
Eyes of brown or blue, which will they be?
She always has this smile for everyone to see.

A joy when you came to us, almost like a toy,
The Lord must have sent you, for us to enjoy.
Your delivery was a problem, something about the cord.
Everything turned out fine; that was the will of the Lord.

With two big sisters to kinda set the pace,
They think you are real special, welcome to the race.
Ready to love and help you any way they can,
Be it playing dolls or maybe digging in the sand.

Mom and Dad saved you for last, that's not all bad.
A bundle like they wanted, hearts were all so glad.
You made three little girls with the last name of Pribble.
When you came along, their happiness was triple.

Your dad is quite famous; he did receive the "Thomas."
Always there for you, this is his promise.
Your mom is famous also, for patience, love, and smile,
She has all other moms beat by a country mile.

These grandparents love you also, always there for you.
Though your name is Jennifer, we lovingly call you
   "who-who."

June1991

Yonder

A voice which only he could hear
Whispered, "Come," close to his ear.
He saddled up and rode away
To find somewhere a fairer day,
With meadows green from gentle rain
Away from earthly strife and pain.
His favorite horse, his trusted pal,
Stands with empty saddle in the corral.
And though we're sad he's gone away,
We know we'll meet again someday
On some high ridge where things are fair.
We know that he'll be waiting there,
At that last round-up God has planned.
We'll meet there in the Promised Land.
With tireless horse of faultless stride,
We'll make that last eternal ride – together.

Mess Hall Trash

I moved to this place about a week ago,
Private room with a bed soft as dough.

The food is what swayed me, three squares a day.
Morning, noon, and night, all on a large tray.

At first I couldn't wait for the server to show,
Pushing that little cart around, all careful and slow.

You would think she was hauling caviar or baked duck,
But when it gets to your table, you are all out of luck.

When breakfast is served, it's always prunes and toast.
Bacon and over easy is what I like most.

Hot or cold cereal with hash browns on the side,
And to get this trash, you have to wait in line.

Twelve is now here, time for the noon meal.
You walk real slow to the mess hall, it ain't no big deal.

Rutabaga casserole, green beans with mushrooms;
    what a deal!
Pretty soon you wonder, where could I go for a meal?

Rice pilaf, orange-glazed beets, baked acorn, and corn,
    give me a break.
I had as soon have baked possum, or boiled snake.

With all this you get coffee, all you can swig.
Pretty soon you are coffee drunk, and ready to jig.

You get through it somehow, and just wait for supper.
You know this meal you must eat, or all night
    you will suffer.

Spinach lasagna with tater tots; God who dreams up this rot?
It's either eat it or starve. I might make it or not.

I'm here in this place to beat the big "C,"
So I can return home again and be free.

To ride those Paint horses, teach them to slide,
Maybe just look at them, or rub their pretty hide.

Just to clean those stalls again would be a treat,
To hear that boss lady fuss would sound so sweet.

The cooking there is always good cowboy style,
Fried potatoes, red beans, with corn bread can
    make me smile.

I might trade all my tomorrows for one yesterday,
If I could stop father time, just let it stay.

With so many great days, which should I choose?
Cutting on Little Gay Doc, feeling those big moves.

Maybe riding Sugar Whiz with her quick little step.
Or at a horse show. What a nice trip.

Whatever day I choose, one thing I know,
My wife will be with me, she makes my day glow.

February 1996

Cowboy Memories

Tonight I sit here thinking of days gone by,
About the trails I have ridden under beautiful skies.
The ranch folks I've known were the very best.
As I think about them, I know I have been blessed.

Watching the seasons change from summer to fall,
Finding a baby calf from a faraway bawl.
See the mother, run to it, all anxious with concern.
Just watching Mother Nature, we have plenty to learn.

Good horses to ride with plenty of savvy and heart.
So willing to please, so agile and smart.
I loved them all; their memories will stay.
There is no thrill to equal a high-stepping bay.

With hat, boots, jeans, and spurs on your heels,
A good horse and saddle, with plenty of feel.
This is cowboy happiness in the highest degree,
Far from city life, with crowds and cars to see.

My one aim in life was not to walk behind a plow.
I wanted to be cowboy, look after some cows.
It wasn't always easy, but my one dream came true,
Most of my life has been spent under skies of blue.

The horses I have ridden, I loved them all.
Just thinking about them, the good ones I recall.
There was little Mollie Bee, I raised her with love.
When cutting a cow, she could float like a dove.

Then there was this Leo - Three Bar mare; I called
    Leona Barbee.
It was never over until she worked, they must wait and see.
She could run wide open, then stop and turn around.
It happened every time, no matter the town.

Miss Prescription was something; I liked her a lot.
She moved so fast, she could shed a bot.
A winner of two buckles the year I showed her,
In front of a cow she became nothing but a blur.

Little Oakie was a double buckle winner also.
Anywhere you worked him, the grass wouldn't grow.
He came out of Oklahoma; his real name was Doc's Najo.
When breeding fine horses, he was the best you can grow.

Another good one was Little Doc's Sweeper.
Bred to be a good one, he was no sleeper.
He would move on a cow and really rattle and shake.
When he turned around, he was just like a snake.

The prettiest one I guess was Gay Doc's Spot.
Of all the one's I trained, I liked him a lot.
He won us a trophy and buckle also.
If I must win a cutting, he is the one I would show.

There was Magic and Roman and Ellie also.
Clear the herd with a cow, then watch them glow.
Just sit up there and ride them with your hand on their neck,
Stay out of their way to avoid a big wreck.

A remember another one was Doc Napco Paint.
The way he could spin, he must have been a saint.
I will never forget a horse we called Big Poco,
A mountain of a horse, but could cut them fast or slow.

The first horse I had, we called Flicka.
Always rode her bareback, but could she sickle.
A pretty bay filly she was, only two years old.
I can still remember that feeling of being free and bold.

When God made man and put him on course,
I'm sure the next thing he loved best was the horse.
You add up both their good points, and what the heck,
It seems the horse won easily by a neck.

Sugar Whiz was the best; she belonged to my wife,
My very first winner, after starting my new life.
A pretty Paint mare, with the big pretty eye,
Seldom ever beaten, she had so much try.

This is just a few that sure left their mark.
I can't recall them all, but they are still in my heart.
There was Trixie, H.C., Skeeter, Bucky, and High Socks,
Chipper, Snipper, Blue, Old Jack, Miss Prescription,
    and Hard Rocks.

God loved them I know, just as much as I did.
With His love and mercy, I will see them again.
When they have that big round-up in the sky,
I will cut out this bunch to ride in that sweet by and by.

July 6, 2000

A Cowboy's Prayer
(written for mother)

Oh Lord, I've never lived where churches grow.
    I've always loved creation better as it stood
That day You finished it so long ago
    And looked upon Your work and called it good.
I know that others find You in the light
    That's sifted down through tinted window panes,
And yet I seem to feel You near tonight
    In this dim, quiet starlight on the plains.

I thank You, Lord, that I am placed so well,
    That You have made my freedom so complete;
That I'm no slave of whistle, clock or bell,
    Nor weak-eyed prisoner of wall and street.
Just let me live my life as I've begun
    And give me work that's open to the sky;
Make me a pardner of the wind and sun,
    And I won't ask a life that's soft or high.

Let me be easy on the man that's down;
    Let me be square and generous with all.
I'm careless sometimes, Lord, when I'm in town,
    But never let 'em say I'm mean or small!
Make me as big and open as the plains,
    As honest as the hawse between my knees,
Clean as the wind that blows behind the rains,
    Free as the hawk that circles down the breeze!

Forgive me, Lord, if sometimes I forget.
    You know about the reasons that are hid.
Just keep an eye on all that's done and said
    And right me, sometimes, when I turn aside,
And guide me on the long, dim trail ahead
    That stretches upward toward the Great Divide.

Badger Clark

Square-Skirted Frazier Saddle

Now I am an old saddle
covered with a thin layer of dust.
Even my old oxbows are layered
with dust.

I am over 100 years old
Spending my last years in this museum.
If those others there only knew,
I've been more places than all of them.

Why I made the trail from Texas to Miles City,
when only three years old, through
Heat, dust, rain, and snow, and
that unbearable Montana cold.

Not many people look at me. I am
weathered, worn, and kind of old.
Of course, I was pretty plain
even when I was built and sold.

Now that first cowboy who got me
was sure filled with pride.
No one would ever realize,
I was just an old cow hide.

I have had a lot of narrow escapes,
throughout my days, Like the time I
was on the back of that old bald-faced bay,
Why he bucked, kicked, snorted, and fell
tore the leather off my right front swell.

And the tears on my cantle where those
Kelly spurs left their marks,
When a horse I was on fell on a cowboy
who was riding hard to stop
a stampede in the dark.

Now I sit here in this room, not to
be rode anymore. Just an old
square-skirted Frazier, an old

relic on a rack bolted to the floor.

I really do not fit among this fine
collection, of hand-tooled silver-mounted
trophies and such. And when you
start comparing, I'm really not worth very much.

But I never complain, because I am of a select few
who made their place in history,
Which is what most saddles never do.
Yes, I'm just an old saddle.

Tuffy Cooper

The Monument Post Office

I started long ago in this little town, just trying to grow.
A place for folks to get their mail, made them glow.
Good news and bad news, you shared it all
Through wars and hard times, you answered the call.

You were there through it all with mail from home.
The only way folks could stay in touch, who had to roam.
More than a Post Office it seems to me.
You have always been a place for old friends to see.

Long ago when everything was real slow
You were a place to discuss the weather or how the kids
   could grow.
The Postmasters who guided you did it in style,
Always so friendly and helpful, they did it with a smile.

There was Helen and Frances and Sandi, to name a few,
Thanks for always being there in the snow, rain, or when the
   wind blew.
So today is your birthday, a hundred years have passed.
My, my, how time flies, they went by so fast.

I feel we have been blessed, for the service you gave,
You have made our lives a little better, this side of the grave.
We will give you all the blame, and the credit, too,
Because, heck, we wouldn't still be a town if it wasn't for you.
Happy 100, Monument Post Office.

Year 2001
Written for the Monument, NM Post Office 100th-Year Anniversary

Happy 100th Anniversary
Monument Post Office

Vernon E. Roberts
2430 Roundup Dr.
Hobbs, NM 88240-2536

CENTENNIAL STAT...
100 YEARS
1900 - 2000
DECEMBER 19, 2000
MONUMENT, NM 88265

The White House

Vernon E. Roberts
2430 Roundup Dr.
Hobbs, NM 88240-2536

Jerry

He is gone from us now, this wonderful man,
Always handled every task thrown him and sure made a hand.
Such a joy to know, I can still hear his laugh.
The ones he loved most were his kids and better half.

A New Mexico cowboy, in his early years
Riding, branding, and breaking, there was no fear.
A bad horse to him was just part of the job.
The neighbor ranchers sure liked him, especially old Bob.

Famous Bob Crosby knew Jerry was the best.
The way Jerry came across to people shows he was blessed.
Growing up on that small, dried-out ranch,
Doing without and getting by, no time to dance.

Working at a clay pit, loading trucks, sometimes by hand,
Then take his money home to feed the whole clan.
Or maybe buy some cows for his mother and dad.
There was never much left for young Jerry, seems sad.

He loved his little brothers and sisters and let it show.
There was always candy and toys at Christmas to make them
    glow.
So unselfish and giving where they were concerned.
If only the others had watched, there was plenty to learn.

Things would get better, this was his plan.
Get an education, so young Jerry took a stand.
Though hard it was, he would not give up.
He would keep at it and succeed, with just a little luck.

This he did. An engineer he became.
I'm sure in the family this gave him some fame.
Being born during the Depression, it was hard to survive.
You just worked and slaved, and tried to stay alive.

At that age and time, educated people were few.
But Jerry achieved this, his opportunities grew.
He did this at a time when living was real hard.

Many a time, I feel, he would call on the Lord.

His fame and fortune would be put on hold.
The Korean War had broke out and began to unfold.
Jerry, like so many, answered the call
To go over and put a stop to that brawl.

The war was over at last, so that page was turned.
Trouble and strife do pass, the lessons we learned.
The ranch life was long gone, just a faint memory.
He would spend his life out with no more cattle to see.

A good job he had, being an engineer and all.
Jerry now had a loving wife and seven kids, I recall.
There was Marilyn his wife, such a pretty thing.
Life was so good and happiness she did bring.

The years passed so fast and just ran right by,
But somehow long ago, Jerry learned to fly.
He was a pilot and loved this so much,
Flying an airplane, raising a family and such.

Seven youngsters they had and how he would brag.
It never seemed to bother him when they would nag.
There was Scott, Mark, Rusty, and John, they would carry his
    name.
Also Cindy, Tina, and Jody, they could do no blame.

Jerry loved them all and they were special to him.
I guess taking care of brothers and sisters made him a gem.
Patience and caring stood him apart.
All the days he lived, he always showed heart.

An unexpected tragedy blew Jerry's life apart.
His youngest son John was taken, this broke his heart.
A train accident took this young man's life.
He was making a crossing which had no signal or light.

Their hearts broken over the loss of a brother and son
Never again to see him in that eighteen-wheeler make his run.
Put a bar at that crossing, was their request.
That won't bring him back, but it might help him rest.

Jerry's last years should have been the best, you would think.
But Mom and Dad had saddled him with a burden, that's the kink.
They made him administrator over all they had.
They trusted Jerry's good judgment, but things turned real sad.

Fair-minded Jerry tried, but it was all in vain.
Misled lawyers and greedy relatives made life a pain.
Nothing went the way Jerry wanted, and this broke his heart.
But rest easy old friend, maybe they weren't that smart.

Dried-out old ranch, with no water or fence,
They gave up some dear brothers, not to mention Sis.
Always so respected for decisions you made.
Things your Mom and Dad wanted was not for trade.

Jerry had this old friend, who was loyal and neat.
When he passed from this life, she was there at his feet.
They would take walks and just visit and such.
Now that Jerry is gone, Amber will miss him so much.

Gone now to that better place of love and grace
Together forever with John, where you set your own pace.
Walk easy, my brother, on those streets of gold.
We will all join you soon, when this life unfolds.

Written for Cindy and Tina,
August 2000

My Brother Melvin

My brother left this world today. It was so hard to say goodbye.
But he has found another place so wonderful, there in the sky.
His heavenly Father will greet him there with a smile on his face.
Old Mel will say "Father I never dreamed of such a beautiful
    place."

His Father will say "Come in, my son, this is all for you.
Here are your friends and family and you don't have to choose.
Up here there is only kindness, peace, and most important, love.
That's about the only rules we have here. Feel free as the dove."

Mel will probably crack a funny or two just for the laugh.
Then I'm sure he will tell them all about the past.
He will tell them about the horses he rode, about the winter and
    fall.
Old Mel was quite a storyteller, as I recall.

What a joy he was here on Earth to the people he loved the most.
Now that he's not here, my heart is so sad, this place is like a
    ghost.
We are all just walking through this life knowing it can't last.
But life up there goes on forever. Won't that be a blast?

Grass stirrup-high with water so pure and blue.
God made all of this so perfect, just for Mel and you.
So walk easy, my brother, in that heavenly place.
We will all be together again when we, too, finish this life's race.

February 26, 2001

Levi - The Cowboy

Levi was with us for such a short time.
The Lord had other things for him to do, in the sky.
God had cows to look after, and colts to ride.
He needed Levi there by His ever-loving side.

Now Levi can ride those colts on that open range
He learned it all here, and that won't change.
A born natural at what he liked to do.
Soft hands and loving care kept them on cue.

Those ole colts can blow up, if they have a mind.
This won't bother young Levi, he's rode every kind.
He will talk to them soft, and use a gentle hand.
Levi knows what it takes to make a horse understand.

A born cowboy while here on this earth.
We will all miss you, for what that's worth.
You will keep that gate up there open wide.
It won't be that long before we're by your side.

We will again enjoy your fun and mischievous ways.
Up there forever, with beautiful new trails to blaze.
Gone from us now, and we will miss you so much.
God's promise will get us through, that's our big lunch.

Our minds are so little; we can't grasp it all.
But in God's word, He will never let us fall.
We will just keep the faith until our time comes,
Enjoy the good times, and forget the crumbs.

It's people here on earth that make the joy.
You was so nice, never fickle or coy.
Up there now, where grass is stirrup-high,
You can ride on forever in that sweet by and by.

March 9, 2006

112

The Broken Chain

We little knew that morning
That God was going to call your name.
In life we loved you dearly.
In death we do the same.

It broke our hearts to lose you,
You did not go alone;
For part of us went with you,
The day God called you home.

You left us peaceful memories.
Your love is still our guide;
And though we cannot see you,
You are always at our side.

Our family chain is broken
And nothing seems the same;
But as God calls us one by one,
The chain will link again.

Written for Bedford Franklin "Buddy" McBryde
Born February 8, 1932
Died March 12, 2007

We Have a Choice

Now it's coming right up, the time to vote.
It's the one freedom we have left, so let's make the most.
We have a sheriff's race here in the county of Lea.
Two good men running, but who will it be?

It takes a really good man who really stands tall
To put himself in harm's way for us all.
He stands right up there between the good and the bad
With very little help from us, seems real sad.

He watches over us while we sleep or play,
Stopping the bad guys from making us their prey.
One of these men, I will give my support
Doing the job anyway, with very good reports.

When you look at other places, and all that's going on,
We have it pretty good here in Lea, as we move along.
Let's keep it that way, and never sway,
So in the future, we can all say:

We did it right this time, with no maybe or might,
This sheriff we all elected, did us up right.
Now all you crooks, low-lifes, and dopies
Better get on the next stage

Because the man you are going to face is Sheriff John Gates.

October 5, 2006

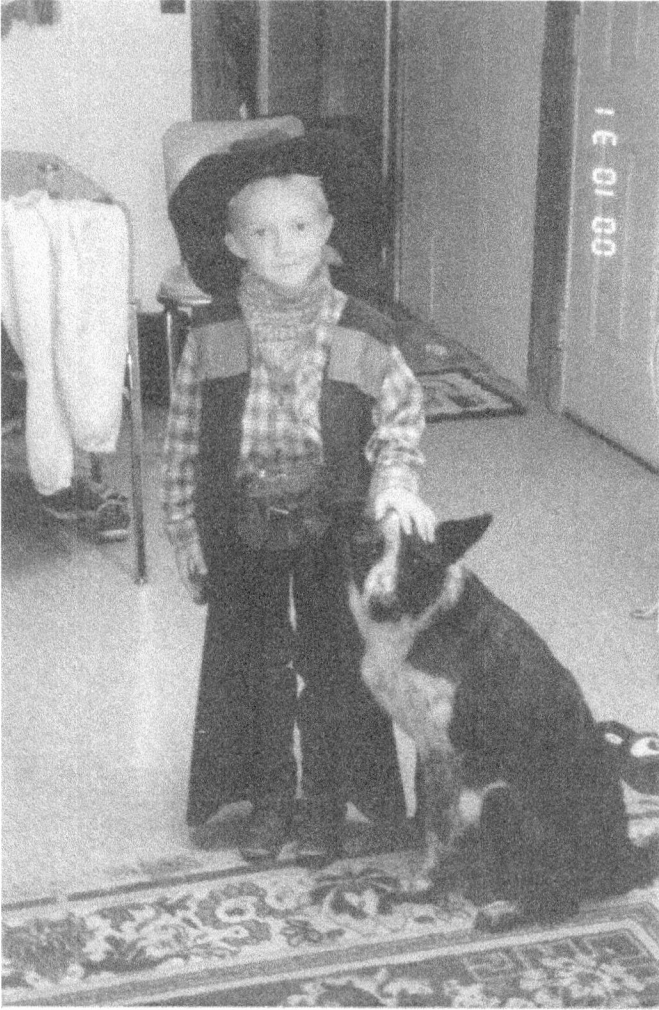

Little Beau, The Wrangler

The littlest cowboy now, but before too long
You will be all grown up, big and strong.
Your Grandpa's been watching you now for a year or more,
You've got all the making of a cowboy for sure.

I can see it in your eyes and the way you walk.
When a cowboy says something, it's not just talk.
It will always be the truth, and worthwhile to hear.
You walk real tall and never show fear.

Your Grandpa's been around for seventy years or more.
I just want to pass on a few things that might help you for sure.
Always take care of your horse. Never be little or mean.
Never ride him when he is hungry. Keep your saddle blanket
    clean.

Remember he gets tired just like you.
Never get him in a bind, watch all the gates you go through.
Keep his feet trimmed or even walking on iron;
Go as fast as you like, but never back to the barn.

He will always be your partner, and stand behind you all the way,
If you show love and consideration, never weave or sway.
Put on this earth just for us, to ride and enjoy,
Such a wonderful animal, never fickle or coy.

You will ride some really good ones as your young life unfolds.
Just remember each one; they will warm you when it's cold.
They are all different, no two are alike.
But they will all claim your heart, be it day or night.

You are such a lucky little cowboy, you know,
And you will realize this as older you grow.
Being born and raised on a ranch and all,
Riding, gathering cattle, and shipping in the fall.

You have a head start over all the rest,
And when it comes down to one on one, you will be the best.
Only about one boy in a million can ever say
They were raised on a ranch, and did it their way.

Cowboying up there in the high country is no easy chore,
But when you go up to bring 'em down, you make a hand for
    sure.
No matter how scattered or hard to find,
Seems you always find them; us cowboys call that kicking
    behinds.

You was named after that great cowboy, Lane Frost.
He was gored by a bull at Cheyenne, we all felt the loss.
Loved by everyone, I guess, nationwide.
He always had a smile, and boy he could ride.

This is your legacy, little cowboy, Beau.
Always be honest and fair as older you grow.
Listen to your Mom and Dad when they have something to say.
They love you and will guide you, if you will just obey.

This is about all I guess your Grandpa has to say.
Except I do love you, I guess that makes my day.
We don't seem to get to be together very much.
But I think of you so often - morning, night, and lunch.

You just keep up the good work, there in those mountains and
    trees.
And may you always know your Grandpa is so proud and pleased.

Love you Beau
Grandpa Leroy
October 13, 2000

The Old Brown Hat Birthday

For Christmas Day last year, we made a trip out West.
After a short visit with the kids, we hopped in the car
For a trip to meet a fine Cowboy poet, one of the best.

A winding road south took us to the land of enchantment
Where coyotes run free and Roadrunners to see
Where one dreams of the past and we see Indian encampments.

On arrival there the greeting was, "Howdy, you'll come on in."
Entering this beautifully reclaimed cabin on Conchas Lake
Leroy and Dolores were so great, we hoped it would never end.

Now Leroy is celebrating a special day in his life we all know
He's a man of God and shares his love in words for all.
There's "The Cowboy, Dolores and Me, and Gay Doc" for show.

This note is for you today, Leroy the "Retired Cowboy." Best
   wishes
My friend and may you have health, happiness, and success.
Feed those ponies, care for your family, and praise God with the
   Mrs.

Happy Birthday Leroy.

Written By Dan Gillis
For Leroy's 80th Birthday
March 12, 2009

Cox and Davis, All in the Blood

Our reunion time is finally here again.
It brings to mind things way back when.
Loved ones who are gone and in the past,
But the love I had for them will last and last.

There was Pete, William, Mother and Daddy, Junior, and Billy
    Emsoft, to name a few,
Uncle Elbert, Aunt Dena, Uncle Bud, Aunt Bernice, and Uncle
    Otis, too.
Uncle Leonard, Aunt Etta, Aunt Ruby, Uncle Jody, still in my
    heart.
I sure can't forget Grandpa Cox, I thought he was so smart.

He was a real cowboy from his head to his toe.
He did it for the love of ranching, not for the dough.
I guess he passed it on, his sons were the same.
Francis and Alford both loved that cowboy game.

These were our loved ones who ran their race.
They have all gone now, to that other place.
I remember them with love for the time we had.
That we were not together more makes me so sad.

That first reunion was at Albany, down on the creek.
I let my mind wander sometimes for one more peek.
John and Bonnie Woodfin, with their son Tuffy for sure.
Little Tuffy almost drowned that day, not far from the shore.

My Daddy, Clyde, saw him go under for the third time.
Without a word to anyone, Daddy swam and got him; he would be
    fine.
We spread our food that day under those big old trees.
No one had very much money, but life seemed a breeze.

There was so much love back then, almost like a flood.
As I think about it now, I know it was in the blood.
Uncles, Aunts, Cousins, Nieces, and Nephews, also,
You loved them all because you knew you were supposed to.

They would spend money to see everyone,
    sometimes they didn't have.
They knew this was the only blood kin they would ever have.
We should be more like these folks, they were our roots.
Maybe we have all become a bunch of old coots.

We come to the reunion if we really want to, it seems.
Or maybe we'll just skip a year or so, just to be mean.
Now let me tell you something, and I'll tell you true.
This is your reunion and it's all up to you.

Let's keep it like it used to be, with love and joy.
Not mess around and play with it, like it's a toy.
Everyone wants to see you, because you are kin.
Then when you get old like us, you can look back when.

Soon all us older ones will be gone and just a memory,
So all you youngsters enjoy it while you can and just maybe,
When you grow old like us you will remember your kin,
You can look back and say, "Those days were a win."

Jason Scott Smith

As I sit here in the old bunk house
And stare at the wall
At all those pictures taken long ago,
When you were so small.

There is one with your little boots, saddle
And hat all tipped back.
I believe your dad wanted you to be
A cowboy, the looks you sure don't lack.

Your trail didn't lead that way, and
Looking back, it's just as well.
All the things you have done since
Would make a Grandpa's head swell.

Magnolia school was where you would go
Such a good student, never lazy or slow.
You played by the books, never broke a rule.
So happy you wanted them to be your school.

It was football for you, the game you loved.
You played it so well it fit like a glove.
It started for you at the age of twelve.
Guard was your spot, you handled it so well.

You could sure handle that hole in the line.
They tried to get by you, they were in a bind.
No one could push you around, they found out.
Big Jason was there and he was too stout.

Your school ended in 1999, I think.
Seems it all went by like a blink.
It was now time to make a choice
No one could help you or lend a voice.

It would be college, go to work, or the Navy.
Those choices sure weren't all gravy.
After much thought, you knew what to do.
You would put on the uniform with the black shoes.

Yes, that pretty Navy blue was for you,
A radio man out there on that ocean of blue,
The USS Anzio and what a ship
An Aegis Class Cruiser, all shiny and hip.

Stationed in old Norfolk was where you would be.
Other places you would go, but just wait and see.
In the Mediterranean at the beginning of Iraq,
You was right in the middle of that pack.

Four years you had served, should be enough.
But you re-enlisted, you could not give up.
Now eight years you have served us all.
Just to try and stop that awful brawl.

You have served us well, Grandson of mine.
I am so proud you are that kind.
May you always be happy and aglow
And the rough times not even stow.

The picture I've seen of your friend, Michelle.
What a pretty girl, the right kind I can tell.
I'm sure she couldn't replace little "Kitty"
Second place ain't that bad, down to the nitty gritty.

I may never say I love you face to face.
But know I do, always, here or that Other Place.
The years pass so fast, I don't see you a lot.
You will always be my first Grandson.
And that does mean a lot.

I love you
Your Grandpa Leroy.
March 31, 2008

Old Jim Cooper

Now Old Jim is kinda long at the tooth, kinda like me.
But don't let that fool you, old Jim still stands like a tree.
Known far and wide and about everywhere
As one of the best ropers to ever strap on a spur.

The first, I have been told, to leave a horse from the right
Ropers had never seen this before, it was quite a sight.
They said, "Jim, you can't do that, this is wrong."
Jim didn't care what they said; he just took their money home.

He was roping really well at this time.
So he decided Old Calgary was the place for his rope to unwind.
This old country boy made that long trip just to see
How he would stack up. Maybe a champion he could be.

Too young and wild to ever know or show fear,
He was riding this good horse, who knew every gear.
Jim won it all that day, so long ago.
From that day forward, his reputation did grow.

Jim was now the North American Roping Champion of the
    World.
He had sure picked the right place to let his rope uncoil.
So many miles and jillions of ropings have since gone by.
Old Jim is still out there roping, with plenty of try.

Now my friend Jim is kinda a temperamental cuss.
But you be fair and square and there will be no fuss.
You treat him wrong or come up short.
Old Jim will sure head you back on course.

He passed his great talent on to his partner and son.
There is no way to know how much money he has won.
All Around World Champion is sure no easy task.
Young Jim did this in the eighties, like he was blessed.

Two young Grandsons now, who can sure hold their own.
Two future World Champions, I predict, before too long.
This is just a few things I wanted you to know.
Old Jim is not always tensile and show.

He is the one person, if I could, I would choose
To be my lifelong friend. He never learned to lose.

January 5, 2001

If This Old Tack Could Talk

The wooden door hangs crooked
On a broken rusty hinge
Bailing wire now holds the latch
Where once a lock had been.

A floor of dust and cinders
Tattered walls and cobwebbed beams.
It's a cowboy's house of treasures
And a horseman's living dream.

Now along one wall are pictures
Of horses, both young and old
Who came to know the hands
And one man's heart and soul.

And these well bred colts and fillies
Learned the ways to prove themselves
As shown by the trophies
Standing tarnished on the shelf.

There's some tiny little halters
In the corner that I found
That the old man put on the babies
Old enough to lead around.

A trunk with hobbles, ropes and twitches
That the cowboy used with care
To breed, or worm, or doctor
When the old vet wasn't there.

The snaffle bits have rusted
Except the inlaid silver rings
On the Mexican creations
That he bought from there, one spring.

But those split reins lay so neatly
On those headstalls in a row
You feel the care that once was taken
By the way they're hung just so.

Hackamores and sidepulls
Almost fill the second wall
So many rawhide wonders
It'd be hard to count them all.

Spades and Mona Lisa bits
Hang stately one by one.
And the silver cheeks still sparkle
As they catch the morning sun.

Tie downs, leads, and drive lines
Woven blankets by the score
And some trick bits, gags, and gadgets
That you just can't find no more.

And the saddles, boys
You'll never see a better bunch
And each one had a special purpose
To that old hand, I have a hunch.

Well it saddens me to be here
Cause the old man's left us now.
Guess the Lord's just short-handed
And needs help to work his cows.

Now he's up there in green pastures
Riding meadows at a walk
And to this young buckaroo
It could mean a lot
If this old tack could just talk.

By Brad Hall
Casper, Wyoming
Reprinted from The Fence Post
March 14, 2005

Haven't Sold Your Saddle

"Not so terribly well," I said, in answer to his question.
"I'm runnin' fast, but wonder if it's in the wrong direction.
My wife has started gainin' weight and gray shows in her hair;
Her existence seems to be in runnin' kids from here to there.

"My job has lost its challenge; it seems like it never changes.
Sometimes I'd like to chuck it all and leave to ride new ranges."
I thought my friend would understand; he'd walked this same ol'
    road
And had made decisions in his life to drop his heavy load.

So, I laid my troubles on him and I told him how I felt.
He just stares at me, all hollow, like he's hit below the belt.
He sits down close, all weak-like, and he looks me in the eye.
His hands, they started tremblin', I believes he's gonna cry.

He swallows hard an' tells me, "I know what you're up against;
It happens at this time of life. You feel like you've been fenced.
Seems like life becomes routine…it all just feels the same,
So, you go to huntin' witches, lookin' for someone to blame.

"Our work and wife scapegoat real well when we are of that mind,
And little faults become big, 'cuz, that is what we want to find.
Please don't make my same mistakes and let a notion be your
    guide.
The grass ain't greener, I see that -- now I'm on the other side.

"I upturned several lives with my leaving, plus my own,
An' lost my common little family and my routine little home.
I'd have never left if I had taken time to figure out
That what I wanted out of, is what life is all about.

"We're seldom taught that, though; seems it's almost out of style.
If I could just have one more chance, I'd walk that extra mile.
But that can't be, now I must lie upon the bed I've made
While my will to carry on, like bad memories, starts to fade.

"And if you never take advice again, please heed these words, my

friend:
The purpose of life's race is in the running to the end.
There will be times it seems so far we fear we'll never make it;
We tire and lose sight of dreams and want to just forsake it.

"It's still all in your mind right now, but thought precedes the act.
And it isn't yet too late, my friend -- I know that for a fact.
You've started your race gamely. You've just been bumped
   against the rail.
I'm not sayin' you sold your saddle, but you've put it up for sale."

Waddie Mitchell
Used by permission
Waddie's Word Publishing

Stuart Hamblen

Back in the 50's there was a well known radio host and song writer in Hollywood named Stuart Hamblen. He was noted for his drinking, womanizing, partying, etc.

One of his bigger hits at the time was "I won't go hunting with you Jake, but I'll go chasing women."

One day, along came a young preacher holding a tent revival. Hamblen had him on his radio show, presumably to poke fun at him. In order to gather more material for his show, Hamblen showed up at one of the revival meetings.

Early in the service, the preacher announced "There is one man in this audience who is a big fake."

There were probably others who thought the same thing, but Hamblen was convinced that he was the one the preacher was talking about (some would call that conviction). But, he was having none of that.

Still, the words continued to haunt him, until a couple of nights later, he showed up drunk at the preacher's hotel door around 2:00 am and demanded the preacher pray for him.

But, the preacher refused, saying, "This is between you and God and I'm not going to get in the middle of it."

But he did invite Stuart in and they talked until about 5:00 am, at which point Stuart dropped to his knees and with tears cried out to God.

But that is not the end of the story. Stuart quit drinking, quit chasing women, and quit everything that was "fun". Soon, he began to lose favor with the Hollywood crowd.

He was fired from the radio station when he refused to accept a beer company as a sponsor.

Hard times were upon him. He tried writing a couple of "Christian" songs, but the only one that had much success was

"This Old House", written for his friend Rosemary Clooney.

As he continued to struggle, a long-time friend named John took him aside and told him, "All your troubles started when you got religion. Was it worth it all?"

Stuart simply answered, "Yes."

Then his friend asked, "You liked your booze so much, don't you even miss it?" His answer was "No." John then said, "I don't know how you could give it up so easily."

Stuart's response was "It's no big secret. All things are possible with God."

To this John said, "That's a catchy phrase. You should write a song about it"

The song Stuart wrote was "It Is No Secret What God Can Do".

It is no secret what God can do.
What He's done for others, He'll do for you.
With arms wide open, He'll welcome you.
It is no secret what God can do.

By the way...
The friend was John Wayne

And the young preacher who refused to pray for Stuart Hamblen?
That was Billy Graham.

Author Unknown

Cindalynn

You are gone now, and we are all so sad,
But the memories of you make everyone so glad.
That sweet laugh will be with us always,
The little sweet things you would do, was just your way.

Father's Day and holidays, you never forgot,
Being just a step-father really meant a lot.
I loved you, little girl with all my heart,
The good-bye was so hard when we had to part.

It helps to know you are there in that heavenly place,
Before too long we will again see that beautiful face.
Up there with those angels who went on before,
Having joy and laughing, having fun galore.

Don't you worry about a thing here on this earth,
Memories of you will see us through, for what that's worth.
Life here we know is not everlasting at all,
But it makes me so sad; you were the first to get the call.

Our Lord knew it was time to call you home,
He gave you some time for these mountains and valleys to roam.
"Come On Up Here, We Need Your Laughter Today,
And We Want To Hear Everything You Have To Say."

You were a fighter, with the heart of a lion.
For so long you had that old disease in a bind.
That old Big C is a cheater and never plays fair,
Its game only causes sadness and despair.

It's gone now, little girl, and can never hurt you again.
When it's all said and done, you showed it how to win.
No more pain, suffering, and strife,
You are there in Heaven now, with your new life.

May God keep you in His gentle hands
Until we will all be together again, in that other land.
Up there with pearly gates, and streets of gold,
And all those other wonders of Heaven will unfold.

132

Jesus made it all possible when He died on that tree.
He saved us for eternity and set our souls free.
If we only believe in him, because he paid the price,
So we could all be together, in that other life.

August 3, 2008

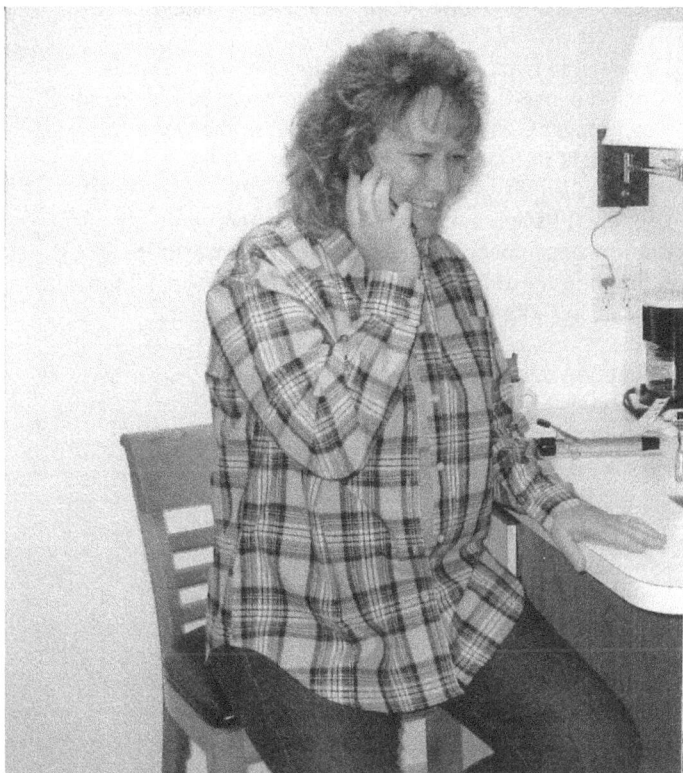

Reverend Dr. Bob Hamilton

You told us all today, that you were going away.
We are all so sad, and wish you could stay.
I know that is selfish on our part to feel that way,
But the words you have taught us are here to stay.

They will long be remembered in these hallowed walls,
About the love God has for us, and to never be little or small.
You brought God's word to us, right from the Good Book.
You taught us to listen, pray, and look.

The time I have known you was just a short while,
But just remembering you can make my heart smile.
A few times preaching from a wheel chair, it was all the same.
You always told folks how to play this life's game.

About how Jesus came down here and
Died on that piece of wood.
How he did it just for us
He showed us all where he stood.

You told us about all these things,
And how we should take a stand.
I have only love and admiration for you,
You sure make a hand.

Though your health is not good, you still have that smile.
Memories like that will sure be with me a while.
God called you long ago, to show us the way,
That we might be together, on that Judgment Day.

Up there together where we will never grow old,
Doing His will, always being brave and bold.
The place you are going, I know is far, far away.
Maybe I will never see you again, is what I'm trying to say.

Should that be God's great plan, we will all see
You again, in that other land.
We will all be good looking, young, and free.
The life ever after will sure be something to see.

Love and happy trails to you and your dear wife.
May your path be straight and smooth
And your every dream come true.

Written 7/14/08
by Cowboy Poet
Leroy Davis

My Cousin

There are many things to say about this good man.
For seventy-nine years my cousin, he was so grand.
A third generation cowboy, his whole life
He did it with pride, no matter the strife.

While still just a kid at the old Matador
He broke those old ranch horses, all threes and fours.
Horses sixteen and seventeen hands, all fully grown.
He was good at his job, seldom, if ever thrown.

He exemplified WHAT IT MEANT, TO RIDE FOR THE
   BRAND.
If he drawed your pay he would make a hand.
It was his great principles that set him apart.
He was never smartalecky, coy, or smart.

Never a big talker about what he could do.
So honest and fair with everyone he knew.
He would never tell a lie even if it hurt.
Those that did were discarded like a dirty shirt.

Picky loved his wife and family with all of his heart,
Always there to see that they got a fair start.
He met his dear wife while at the old turtle hole camp.
Together all those years makes them both a champ.

Taking care of his sister through some bad times,
Even when his own health began to decline.
Together until the end he showed her brotherly love,
Parted now for a little while, but they will always have love.

A born again Christian, we know that for sure.
You loved by God's rules, he would not ask for more.
We will miss you old cousin, and that's a fact,
But you are in a better place, we could not ask you back.

God called you to your wonderful new home,
He has new mountains and valleys for you to roam.
Times here you spent with us was well spent,

But we wonder now where all the time went.

When you enjoy your life seems time can fly.
Praise God before too long we will all be
In that sweet By and By.

Thanks for the memories you gave all of us.
We lived all those years and never had a fuss.
Just being your cousin was a thrill and a joy
When we became grown men, and when we were just boys.

Written 9/11/08
by Leroy Davis

Sam Bruton

My friend Sam was called home
Today, and what a shock.
In my life, for two decades or
More, he had always been like a rock.

We will all miss that sweet smile
And the way you would talk.
The demeanor you always had
And that old cowboy walk.

We go through this life, and the
Trails are not that long.
Before we meet our Jesus, there
On His heavenly throne.

You got to go first old friend
So walk slow and kinda wait for me.
That great roundup up there will
Sure be something to see.

Any time your neighbors had a
Big cow work planned,
You were the one they called, because
At working cows, you were simply grand.

That smile on your face made
Everyone feel great.
No matter the long hours or the
Dirt, dragging calves, or watch that gate.

You did it in style, the real cowboy way.
God has a plan for us all, and
We know here on earth we can't
Always stay.

He will call us home one by one
When our life here has made its run.
We can't know his plan or what's in store,
But He's never made a mistake, that's for sure.

Penny and Bobby Sam, you gave
Him so much joy.
Just know in your heart he
Will be with you forever more.

Just know in your heart he is
Happy and gay.
Because he has gone on
To be with his sweet wife, Faye.

8-17-09
Written by Cowboy Poet
Leroy Davis

Special Brother

A brother is a person you look to when you are in trouble.
   He will give you his last dime or help you in a scuffle.
You spend your first years together and they go by so fast.
   As you get older and look back on life, you wish for the past.
You have a feeling in your heart for him like no other.
   Whether he is older or younger, he is still that special brother.
Through life there are many mistakes, and you make your life part
   of them.
This doesn't change his love for you, because that's the way it
   is,
That's him.
   No I would never change him, not even a little bit.
He is my special brother, who has meant more than life to me.
   How lucky can you get!
We have fought together, played together, and been duty bound.
   My heart is so heavy, and my life has so changed
Now that my brother is not around.
   He has his own family now, and we have both left home.
Many years and miles have passed since we started to roam.
   Years and miles just keep passing, but they can never erase
The fun and love we shared in that other time and other place.
   I remember it all so well, the way he would laugh,
The funny things he could say, still, we can't turn back time.
   So we live our lives day by day.
I will always feel my life has been a little richer because of you.
   It would make my life complete to know that
Well, maybe you felt this way too.

Leroy Davis - After I'm Gone

A pine box will be fine, just simple and plain.
This life was sure fine, but I've broke the chain.
No more heartaches, suffering, or pain,
I go to my new home, my rewards to claim.

Jesus paid the price that I might live again,
Up there forever with Jesus, my new life will begin.
All those loved ones, who went on before
Just waiting to see me; on that heavenly floor.

Mother and Daddy will be there waiting for me.
What a happy time there in heaven, that will be.
Cinda, Joey, and William, and all who have gone on before,
Not to forget those grandparents, who had love galore.

Just thankful for this life and the love I was shown,
I know we will all be together, before too long.
Live the remainder of your life for Jesus each day,
Never let old Satan make your life sway.

The rewards up there are too great to lose
Be careful of worldly things, and the friends you choose.
Live each day like it will be your last,
Keep God ever close. Time goes so fast.

Don't grieve for me, my precious ones.
Life here with you was always so much fun.
Ups and downs we had, sure were a plenty,
And mistakes I made were a way too many.

I can't undo them; you can't relive the past,
But with God's grace, I'm forgiven, my sins are smashed.
I'm here in Glory Land, up here so high.
There is no place on earth like here in the sky.

Just know I love you all with a heart that's true,
Don't let my leaving make your lives blue.
We will all be together again before too long,
I will be waiting and watching, so never do wrong.

October 8, 2008

141

Living for Jesus

Life is uncertain.
Death is for sure.
What would you give to walk
On that heavenly floor?

Would you praise and love God
Every day;
Walk the good life
And never sway?

Reject the old devil and
His wicked ways;
Walk the straight and narrow
And never sway?

Love everybody,
As you do yourself.
Help the poor and rejected
When they need your help.

Always praise Jesus.
He paid the price
So for you and me
This life would be nice.

Heartaches and troubles sometimes come along,
Take that stuff to Jesus, it will be long gone.
You will never have a friend so kind and true.
He is the same every day, because he loves you.

Sometimes we fall short as to what God wants us to be.
He knew this in the garden, when they ate from that tree.
But he is a true and loving God, and he will forgive.
If we just ask, he will always help us to live.

That mansion is just waiting there in the sky.
I pray to be ready when Jesus asks me to fly.
Have I done his will while down here?
When the time comes, will I go with no fear?

Just to see all those loved ones, who went on before.

142

What joy we will have, on that heavenly floor.
Uncles and aunts, Mother and Dad;
Up there together; never troubled or sad.

Just use me, sweet Jesus, with what time I have left.
Put more love in my heart, like I have never felt.
Let me do something to show my love,
Put it on me, Jesus, from heaven above.

January 24, 2009

Just a Whisper Away

No matter how dejected or bad you think you have been
Jesus has always been there, since a way back when.
He is always ready to forgive, and let you start anew.
All you have to do is ask him, and receive your place in skies of
  blue.

He has always been there for you, just a whisper away.
Ready and willing to forgive you and he will never sway.
He said, "Come to me, and I will give you rest."
The best offer I ever heard, this deal is the best.

I just love the verse in John 3:16,
And all the other Bible verses in between.
But this one really caught my eye.
When I think about it, I could almost cry.

"Who so ever believes in me, shall not perish, but have
  everlasting life."
That cuts in my heart and soul like a knife.
To think he died on that cross for you and me.
Some people still reject him and refuse to see.

The price has been paid, so it's all up to you. He left it up to you
  to choose.
Jesus loves us all, with a heart that's so true. He will never force
  you to accept him.
He wants you to love and choose. It is so important for you here
  today
To step out and accept him, and never sway.

Do this now before you start to decay.
Always know that Jesus is just a whisper away.
There is no other way to be with Jesus and be saved for eternity.
Just do it now, and be saved for that great futurity.

If you do it publicly it will make him so glad.
Putting it off for a while will make him so sad.
"If you confess me publicly I will confess you to my Father."
The offer is just as good now as it was then my brother.

Life is but a vapor so it will be over soon.
If you have Jesus in your life there will be no gloom.
Eternity is a long-long time my friend.
Don't wait too long for your decision to begin.

Your life could change this very day.
Jesus loves us all and will never sway.
He has always been there both night and day.
He has always been just a whisper away.

Written by Cowboy Poet
Leroy Davis
August 2009

Leroy's Cowboy Prayer

Lord, I know I am the most uneducated man
To ever pick up a pen,
But with your divine guidance and help
We can show the world how to win.

Just help me put in words what I
Need to say
About sweet Jesus and the awful
Price he was willing to pay.

He paid that high price when they
Nailed him to that piece of wood.
Surely we would change all of that
Now, if we had the power and could.

We all want to do good and do the best
We can; do your will,
But seems we always come up short
And lack the skill.

Seems we all pray to you when times
Get tough.
Then forget it all when everything
Is good and everything is enough.

Lord, you have blessed this nation with
Blessings galore.
Just lead and show us how to
Get it back like it was before.

We came up short and against your
Will, with slavery and all,
But that all changed with your help,
Through old Honest Abe, I recall.

We are living too fast with little
Thought about Jesus and You.
Just help us be more gracious
And thankful for all the things you do.

All those people, who only want to
Kill, cripple, and mame.
Just put more love in their
Hearts, and show them the shame.

We are all brothers here on your
Good Earth.
I wonder why we can't act that
Way, for what that's worth.

Jesus said for us to love one
Another, as we do our self.
Help us be more loving and
Caring for those who need our help.

Just guide and direct me on
This long trail I ride,
And if and when you need me
Give me no place to hide.

Leroy Davis
9/26/2009

This Old Man

You don't get the respect you once
Did, being an old wore out man.
Everyone seems to forget you were once
Young and could sure make a hand.

You yearn for that time you were
Young and every day was a challenge
Now it seems just getting up and
Going is a real battle.

Your legs seem so weak and your
Balance is all gone.
Seems everything you try to
Do is all wrong.

Use to, you could run and play
And work just fun.
Now it's take everything real slow
And easy, and don't dare try to run.

Seems the only thing that stays the same
Is your memories, and that could be a shame.
As you settle in and remember and
Play this old man game.

Being a cowboy to me was the only
Way to go.
Those old broncs never bothered me if
They wanted to blow.

Just get up there and ride them
And show them who was boss.

Working cattle, building fence, checking
Water was just part of the job.
Open country, blue skies, riding a good
Horse, far away from the mob.

These are just some of the things I
Think about, when I let my thoughts remember.

Many miles and years have gone by
Since my life was so tender.

The Lord has always blessed me in
So many different ways. The credit is all His.
I know in my heart he was always
With me back then, and He still is.

I look forward to when I will be
All young again and walk those streets of gold.
I can even run again if I choose to,
In that wonderful place where you never
Grow old.

Leroy Davis
9/26/09

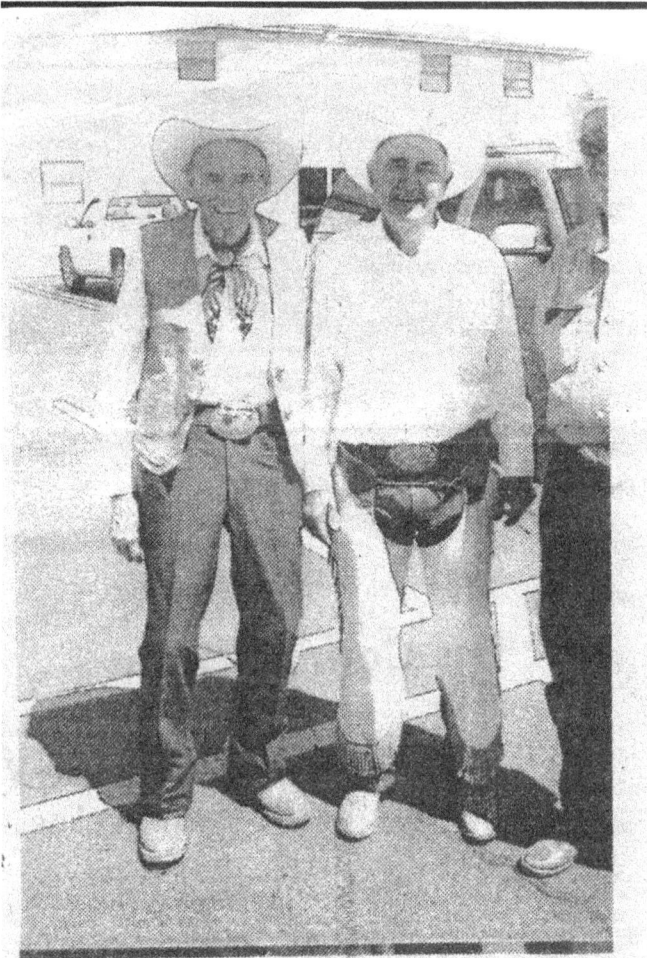

Cowboy Poets give their kind of poetry at the Western Gospel Hour on Sept. 1 2006 at Fellowship of Believers.

www.ingramcontent.com/pod-product-compliance
Lightning Source LLC
Chambersburg PA
CBHW021154160426
42812CB00082B/3007/J